Psychoanalytically Oriented Criticism
of Three American Poets:
Poe, Whitman, and Aiken

Other books by the author:

poetry
rhymed and unrhymed
follow-up

Psychoanalytically Oriented Criticism
of Three American Poets:
Poe, Whitman, and Aiken

Arthur Lerner

Rutherford • Madison • Teaneck
Fairleigh Dickinson University Press

Associated University Presses, Inc.
Cranbury, New Jersey 08512

SBN: 8386 7533 6
Printed in the United States of America

The material on pp. 55, 76 is from *The Basic Writings of Sigmund Freud,* trans. and ed. by Dr. A. A. Brill, Copyright 1938 by Random House, Inc., Copyright renewed 1965 by Gioia Bernheim and Edmund Brill. Reprinted by permission.

The author wishes to thank International Universities Press, Inc., for permission to quote from Gustav Bychowski, "Walt Whitman: A Study in Sublimation," in *Psychoanalysis and the Social Sciences,* Vol. III, ed. Géza Róheim. Copyright 1951 by Géza Róheim, Ph.D., and used with International Universities Press, Inc.'s permission.

The author also wishes to thank The University of Chicago Press for permission to quote from James E. Miller, Jr., *A Critical Guide to Leaves of Grass.* Copyright © 1957 by The University of Chicago Press. Also for permission to quote from Kenneth Burke, "Freud— and the Analysis of Poetry," in the *American Journal of Sociology* 45, 1939. Copyright 1939 by The University of Chicago Press and reprinted from the book *Psychoanalysis and Literature,* edited by Hendrik M. Ruitenbeek. Copyright © 1964 by Hendrik M. Ruitenbeek. Reprinted by permission of E. P. Dutton & Co. Inc.

to
Matilda

Contents

Preface	9
Acknowledgments	11
Introduction	23
The Problem and its Importance	25
Definitions of Terms Used	25
Scope of the Study	27
Organization of the Study	27
1 *Historical and Literary Patterns:*	
Freud in America	29
Psychoanalytically Oriented Literary	
Criticism in the United States	31
Psychoanalysis and Poetry	34
2 *Edgar Allan Poe*	43
Attempts to Study Poe Psychoanalytically	43
Psychoanalytically Oriented Criticism	
of Selected Poe Poetry	47
3 *Walt Whitman*	63
Some Psychodynamic Considerations of	
Whitman	63
Psychoanalytically Oriented Criticism of	
Selected Whitman Poetry	68
4 *Conrad Aiken*	84
Aiken's Relationship to Depth Psychology	84

Aiken's Concept of Beauty and Awareness and
   His Psychoanalytic Insights into
   Selected Poetry   94

5 *Conclusion*   108

Bibliography   113

Index   123

Preface

I have benefited from many sources in the planning, development, and completion of this study. Of great importance in the writing of this manuscript has been the encouragement and guidance given to me by Dr. John W. Nichol and Dr. Robert B. Kaplan, respectively of the English and Linguistic Departments of the University of Southern California. They, along with Dr. Réné F. Bellé of the French Department at the University of Southern California, read and commented upon the original manuscript. Their suggested revisions steered me on my course toward the completion of this project.

Robert J. Lince, M.D., a practicing psychoanalyst, allowed me the use of his extensive library, and provided me with the opportunity to act as a devil's advocate for many theoretical sides of psychoanalysis.

Dr. Nah Brind, psychotherapist and linguist, kept a critical eye on this work and from the vantage point of his vast scholarship helped to clarify my thinking on the relationship between depth psychology and literature.

Helen W. Azhderian, Reference Librarian at the University of Southern California; James F. Saunders, Librarian, Literature Department, Los Angeles Public Library; Mrs. Gwendolyn Roessler Balitzer and Dr. John Nomland, both Professors of Library Services at Los Angeles City College, were extremely generous with their

9

time and patience in locating unlikely sources of information.

Dr. Charles Angoff, Editor of *The Literary Review* and Editor of Fairleigh Dickinson University Press, was most considerate in encouraging me to submit the original manuscript. My editor, Mrs. Mathilde E. Finch, was of tremendous help in shaping the manuscript in its final form. My wife, Matilda, typed the manuscript with meticulous care and patience.

Finally, I wish to make it clear that the final product, whatever its merits, is fully my own responsibility.

Acknowledgments

Grateful acknowledgment is made to the following for permission to quote from previously published material:

Gay Wilson Allen, for permission to quote from Gay Wilson Allen, *Walt Whitman Handbook*. Copyright, 1946, Packard and Company.

American Imago, and to George B. Wilbur, Editor and copyright holder, for permission to quote from Paul Lauter, "Walt Whitman: Lover and Comrade," *American Imago* 16, Winter 1959.

The American Mercury, for permission to quote from Joseph Wood Krutch, "The Strange Case of Poe," *The American Mercury* 6, November 1925.

Appleton-Century-Crofts, for permission to quote from George F. Whicher, "The Twentieth Century," in Arthur Hobson Quinn, ed. *The Literature of the American People: An Historical and Critical Survey*. Copyright 1951, Meredith Corporation. Reprinted by permission of Appleton-Century-Crofts.

A. S. Barnes & Company, Inc., for permission to quote from Conrad Aiken, *Sheepfold Hill*, published by Sagamore Press. Copyright © by Conrad Aiken, 1945, 1946, 1949, 1952, 1958.

Basic Books, Inc., for selections from *The Collected Papers of Sigmund Freud*, edited by Ernest Jones, M.D., Basic Books, Inc., Publishers, New York, 1959.

November 6, 1961. The lecture was printed by Cambridge University Press and published by Leeds University Press, 1962.

Harcourt, Brace & World, Inc., for permission to quote from *Modern Man in Search of a Soul* by C. G. Jung, translated by W. S. Dell and Cary F. Baynes. First published in 1933.

Harper & Row, Publishers, and to Frances Winwar, for permission to quote from Frances Winwar, *American Giant: Walt Whitman and His Times,* Harper & Brothers Publishers. Copyright 1941 by Frances Winwar Grebanier.

Hendricks House, Inc., for permission to quote from Gay Wilson Allen, *Walt Whitman Handbook.* Copyright 1946, Packard and Company.

The Hogarth Press Ltd., for permission to quote from *The Interpretation of Dreams* I (1900) Vol. 4 and *The Interpretation of Dreams* II and *On Dreams* (1900–1901) Vol. 5; "Creative Writers and Day-Dreaming" in Vol. 9; "On the History of the Psycho-Analytic Movement" in Vol. 14; "Psycho-Analysis" in Vol. 18; *Civilization and Its Discontents* in Vol. 21; *New Introductory Lectures on Psycho-Analysis* in Vol. 22; to Sigmund Freud Copyrights Ltd., the Institute of Psycho-Analysis and The Hogarth Press Ltd. for permission to quote from *The Standard Edition of the Complete Psychological Works of Sigmund Freud,* revised and edited by James Strachey. Also, for selections from Marie Bonaparte, *The Life and Works of Edgar Allan Poe: A Psycho-Analytic Interpretation,* translated by John Rodker. First English edition, 1949. Copyright by Imago Publishing Co., Ltd., 1949. (Available in the United States from Humanities Press Inc., who distribute it by arrangement with The Hogarth Press Ltd.) One of the quotations also ap-

Louisiana State University Press, for permission to quote from Frederick J. Hoffman, *Freudianism and the Literary Mind.* Copyright © 1945, 1957. Also to Grove Press, Inc., First Evergreen Edition, 1959.

The Macmillan Company, for permission to quote from *The 20's: American Writing in the Postwar Decade,* 2d. ed. by Frederick J. Hoffman. Copyright © 1949, 1953, 1954, 1955, 1962 by Frederick J. Hoffman. The Free Press, a division of The Macmillan Company; for permission to quote from *Hidden Patterns: Studies in Psychoanalytic Literary Criticism* by Leonard and Eleanor Manheim, editors. Copyright © 1966 by The Macmillan Company; and for permission to quote from *The Poetic Mind* by Frederick Clarke Prescott, Copyright 1922 by The Macmillan Company.

David McKay Company, Inc., for permission to quote from Houston Peterson's *The Melody of Chaos.* Copyright 1931 by Longmans, Green and Co.

William Morrow & Company, Inc., for permission to quote from Richard Chase, *Walt Whitman Reconsidered,* William Sloane Associates, Inc. Copyright © 1955 by Richard Chase.

New York University Press, for permission to quote from Vernon Hall, Jr. Reprinted by permission of the publisher from *A Short History of Literary Criticism,* by Vernon Hall, Jr., © 1963 by New York University, and to The Merlin Press Ltd. for British Commonwealth rights.

W. W. Norton & Company, Inc., for quotations from Sigmund Freud, *Civilization and Its Discontents,* newly translated from the German and Edited by James Strachey. Copyright © 1961 by James Strachey; also for quotations from Sigmund Freud, *New Introductory Lectures on Psycho-Analysis,* translated from the orig-

Richard Blackmur, "The Day Before the Daybreak," which first appeared in *Poetry*, April 1932. Copyrighted 1932 by The Modern Poetry Association and reprinted by permission of the Editor of *Poetry*.

Laurence Pollinger Limited and the Estate of the late Mrs. Frieda Lawrence for permission to quote from D. H. Lawrence, *Studies in Classic American Literature*, William Heinemann Limited, 1961.

Prentice-Hall, Inc., for permission to quote from Walter Sutton, *Modern American Criticism*. Copyright © 1963 by the Trustees of Princeton University. Reprinted by permission of Prentice-Hall, Inc., Englewood Cliffs, New Jersey.

Princeton University Press, for permission to quote from Roy Harvey Pearce, *The Continuity of American Poetry*. Copyright © 1961 by Princeton University Press.

The Psychoanalytic Review, for permission to quote from A. A. Brill, "Poetry as an Oral Outlet." Reprinted from *The Psychoanalytic Review* Vol. XVIII, No. 4, October 1931, through the courtesy of the Editors and the Publisher, National Psychological Association for Psychoanalysis, New York, N.Y. Also for permission to quote from David M. Rein, "Conrad Aiken and Psychoanalysis." Reprinted from *The Psychoanalytic Review* Vol. 42, No. 4, 1955, through the courtesy of the Editors and the Publisher, National Psychological Association for Psychoanalysis, New York, N.Y.

Random House, Inc., and Alfred A. Knopf, Inc., for permission to quote from Harry Levin, *The Power of Blackness*. Alfred A. Knopf, Inc., Copyright © 1958 by Harry Levin, and for permission to quote from J. S. Van Teslaar, *An Outline of Psychoanalysis*. Random House, Inc. Copyright, 1924, by Boni & Liveright, Inc.; Copyright, 1925, by the Modern Library, Inc. Also for

tions 1945–1960 by Evie Allison Allen. Copyright ©
1961 by Southern Illinois University Press.

The Texas Quarterly, for permission to quote from Rufus
A. Blanshard, "Pilgrim's Progress: Conrad Aiken's Poetry," *The Texas Quarterly* 1, No. 4, Winter 1958, by
permission of the author, Rufus A. Blanshard, and the
University of Texas.

Twayne Publishers, Inc., for permission to quote from
Vincent Buranelli, *Edgar Allan Poe,* Copyright © 1961
by Twayne Publishers, Inc.; for permission to quote
from Frederick J. Hoffman, *Conrad Aiken,* Copyright
© 1962 by Twayne Publishers, Inc.; and for permission
to quote from James E. Miller, Jr., *Walt Whitman,*
Copyright © 1962 by Twayne Publishers, Inc.

University of Illinois Press, for permission to quote from
Lorine Pruette, "A Psycho-Analytical Study of Edgar
Allan Poe," *American Journal of Psychology* 31, Oc-
tober 1920.

University of Minnesota Press, for permission to quote
from Joseph Warren Beach, *Obsessive Images: Symbolism in Poetry of the 1930's and 1940's,* edited by William
Van O'Connor. © Copyright 1960 by the University of
Minnesota. And for permission to quote from Richard
Chase, *Walt Whitman.* University of Minnesota Pamphlets on American Writers, Number 9. © Copyright
1961 by the University of Minnesota. Also for permission to quote from Reuel Denney, *Conrad Aiken.* University of Minnesota Pamphlets on American Writers,
Number 38. © Copyright 1964 by the University of
Minnesota.

The University Press of Virginia, for permission to quote
lines from the following verses by Edgar Allan Poe: "A
Dream," "A Dream Within a Dream," "Al Aaraaf,"

Psychoanalytically Oriented
Criticism
of Three American Poets:
Poe, Whitman, and Aiken

Introduction

Generally agreed to be the "father of psychoanalysis,"
Sigmund Freud (1856–1939) developed his theories during a dynamic era of civilization which witnessed tremendous economic, political, and social upheavals. Occurring
during Freud's lifetime were such events as the Franco-
Prussian War, the Russo-Japanese War, the early and
later Russian Revolutions, the Great Depression of the
1930s, and World War I. All these and more are but grim
reminders of the chaos experienced by mankind during
the latter half of the nineteenth century and the first third
of the twentieth century. Also, at the time of Freud's
death, World War II was about to break out with the full
involvement of all the human passions he had been scientifically analyzing for years.

The scientific aspects of psychoanalysis were developed
during a period of world history against a background of
Darwinian evolutionary theory, Marxian economics, and
Einstein's ushering in of the atomic age. Freud's theory of
personality development, particularly its emphasis on
childhood experience as being a major determiner of later
adult neurotic behavior, was quite in keeping with the
scientific spirit of cause and effect prevailing during his
lifetime. And it was in keeping with the spirit of such an
intellectual milieu that psychoanalysis began to make itself felt in many disciplines, including literature.

A long-standing interest in literature and psychoanalysis has led me to the belief that both fields have much to contribute to each other, particularly if they respect one another's potential and limitation.

This respect, of course, has not always been present. Too often, the individual employing psychoanalytic findings to illuminate his literary understanding has forgotten that psychoanalysis is only one branch of dynamic psychology, that it has a rationale of its own, and that the subject-matter of psychoanalysis is not merely involved with pathology or individual psychology. Its interest is in all phases of human behavior.

On the other hand, the individual employing literary works to illuminate his understanding of psychoanalysis has often failed to remember that a character in a play, novel, poem, or in any other literary genre is not a patient on a couch, is not the "classical case." Hence, he too has been responsible for much of the confusion that exists in the attempt to bring the disciplines of literature and psychoanalysis into closer harmony.[1]

Actually, the relationship between literature and the study of human behavior is as old as civilization. The holy books of all nations, sagas, epics, and fairy tales endeavor to depict man's reactions in different settings, in different ways. In recent years, however, psychoanalysis has provided sophisticated tools with which to study and to understand human behavior. Hence, its influence has been widely felt in many fields.

My specific interest in literature lies in the genre of poetry, particularly American poetry. This interest, com-

---

1. Two papers having a direct bearing on this topic are the following: Leon Edel, "Notes on the Use of Psychological Tools in Literary Scholarship," *Literature and Psychology* 1 (September 1951) : 1–3; and William J. Griffin, "The Use and Abuse of Literature," *Literature and Psychology* 1 (September 1951) : 3–20.

bined with an interest in psychoanalysis, has led to a study of the lives and works of Edgar Allan Poe, Walt Whitman, and Conrad Aiken, an excellent trio for study in that they represent both the nineteenth century and the twentieth century. Furthermore, these poets have commanded considered judgment in psychoanalytic literature because of their rich material for psychoanalytic criticism.

THE PROBLEM AND ITS IMPORTANCE

The purpose of this study is exploratory in nature. It aims to learn how selected psychoanalytically oriented critics attempt to understand the works of three American poets, Poe, Whitman, and Aiken.

A search through the literature finds no study of this kind. The trend of applying psychoanalytic understanding to various genres has grown immensely during recent years. This experience, of course, has included the field of poetry. Poe, Whitman, and Aiken have had much critical work of a psychoanalytical orientation done on their poetry. But nowhere has this experience involving these three poets been brought together in an organized fashion. Hence, a study of this kind could lead to a clear understanding of how psychoanalytically oriented criticism functions. This could ultimately result in suggested guidelines for further study and provide a clearer rationale of what the psychoanalytically oriented critic does or does not do in the genre of poetry.

DEFINITIONS OF TERMS USED

The use of the term psychoanalytically oriented criticism is kept within a liberal Freudian framework. The follow-

ing comments serve to elaborate upon the definition of-
fered here. First, there is the point made by Sigmund
Freud himself:

> The assumption that there are unconscious mental proc-
> esses, the recognition of the theory of resistance and re-
> pression, the appreciation of the importance of sexuality
> and of the Oedipus complex—these constitute the prin-
> cipal subject-matter of psycho-analysis and the founda-
> tions of its theory.[2]

There is room in the above quotation for schools of psychoanalysis other than the Freudian. Any school of psycho-
analysis, be it Jungian, Adlerian, and/or various neo-
offshoots, can find a place here in contemporary criticism
if they do what Lee T. Lemon has suggested: ". . . to
explain the genesis of individual poems or of poetry in
general, to interpret the work, and to evaluate it."[3]

In light of the above comments, psychoanalytically
oriented criticism as defined here consists of that theory
primarily developed by Freud, his contemporaries, and
followers which does one or more of these things: (1)
assumes unconscious mental processes, (2) recognizes the
theory of resistance, repression, and other Freudian mechanisms, and (3) appreciates the importance of sexuality
and the Oedipus complex.

---

2. "Psycho-Analysis," in *Miscellaneous Papers, 1888–1938,* ed. James
Strachey, vol. 5 of *Collected Papers,* The International Psycho-Analytical
Library, ed. Ernest Jones, no. 37 (London: The Hogarth Press and the
Institute of Psycho-Analysis, 1950) , p. 122. Also, Sigmund Freud, "Psycho-
Analysis" in *Beyond the Pleasure Principle, Group Psychology, and Other
Works,* vol. 18 (1920–1922) of *The Standard Edition of the Complete
Psychological Works of Sigmund Freud,* rev. and ed. James Strachey (Lon-
don: The Hogarth Press and the Institute of Psycho-Analysis, 1955) , p.
247. I am indebted to Louis Fraiberg, *Psychoanalysis & American Literary
Criticism* (Detroit: Wayne State University Press, 1960) , p. 239 for pointing out this definition.
3. *The Partial Critics* (New York: Oxford University Press, 1965) , p. 91.

SCOPE OF THE STUDY

In the pursuit of this study, the following limitations prevail:

1. The focus of this study is on what selected psychoanalytically oriented critics have to say about selected poems of the three poets under discussion.

2. The stress is on what these selected critics have to say about the works of the poets under consideration or about the poets through their works. Abnormal behavior patterns are not the main concern here, unless the critics themselves bring this out in their criticism.

3. No attempt is made to evaluate the merits of a critic's particular psychoanalytic persuasion.

4. The emphasis here is on explanation. Hence, this study is primarily exploratory in nature.

ORGANIZATION OF THE STUDY

Chapter 1 surveys background information pertinent to the present study. This includes Freud's only visit to the United States, which established the "formal" entrance of his theory upon American territory. This chapter briefly reviews selected psychoanalytically oriented patterns of literary criticism in the United States. And finally, this chapter concerns itself with especially selected material on psychoanalysis and poetry, which will provide a larger frame of reference than the later specifically psychoanalytically oriented literary criticism dealing with each poet.

Chapter 2 presents a discussion of selected psychoanalytically oriented criticism of Edgar Allan Poe. The focus is on what selected critics have said about Poe and/or his poetry, through a study of his poems.

Chapter 3 presents a discussion of selected psychoanalytically oriented criticism of Walt Whitman. The focus is on what selected critics have said about Whitman and/or his poetry, through a study of his poems.

Chapter 4 presents a discussion of selected psychoanalytically oriented criticism of Conrad Aiken. The focus is on what selected critics have said about Aiken and/or his poetry, through a study of his poems.

Chapter 5 presents conclusions and summarizes this discussion of psychoanalytically oriented criticism.

1

Historical and Literary Patterns: Freud in America

In December 1908, Freud was invited by G. Stanley Hall, a distinguished psychologist in his own right and the then President of Clark University, to participate in ceremonies marking the twentieth anniversary celebration of the school.[1] Jung also received an invitation to attend the ceremonies in Worcester, Massachusetts. Both men lectured at Clark University in German in September 1909, Freud delivering five lectures and Jung delivering three.[2] It is interesting to note Freud's reactions. He writes:

> To our great surprise, we found the members of that small but highly esteemed University for the study of education and philosophy so unprejudiced that they

1. Those interested in Freud's only visit to the United States will find the following references helpful: Sigmund Freud, "History of the Psychoanalytic Movement," in *The Basic Writings of Sigmund Freud,* trans. and ed. A. A. Brill (New York: Random House, Inc., 1938), pp. 946–58; A. A. Brill, "The Introduction of Freud's Work in the United States," *American Journal of Sociology* 45 (1939) : 318–25; and Ernest Jones, *The Life and Work of Sigmund Freud* (New York: Basic Books, Inc., 1955), 2: 53–66.

2. The five lectures that Freud delivered were translated by Harry W. Chase, then a Fellow in psychology at Clark University and later Chancellor of New York University. They appeared as "The Origin and Development of Psychoanalysis," *American Journal of Psychology* 21 (April 1910) : 181–218. Jung's lectures were translated by A. A. Brill as "The Association Method," *American Journal of Psychology* 21 (April 1910) : 219–69.

were acquainted with all the literature of psycho-analysis and had given it a place in their lectures to students. In prudish America it was possible, in academic circles at least, to discuss freely and scientifically everything that in ordinary life is regarded as objectionable.[3]

While the above comments by Freud are hopeful signs for freedom of expression on American soil, they in no wise meant that theories of psychoanalysis were to be accepted in the United States without rigorous scrutiny. Neither did they mean that psychoanalytic influences in other fields would be easily accepted. But it was not long before psychoanalytic thinking made itself felt in many fields, one of them being literature.[4] Frederick J. Hoffman's landmark work, *Freudianism and the Literary Mind,* originally published in 1945, traces the psychoanalytic movement in literature through the twenties and into the thirties.

3. Sigmund Freud, "On the History of the Psycho-Analytic Movement" in *On the History of the Psycho-Analytic Movement; Papers on Metapsychology; and Other Works,* vol. 14 (1914–1916) of *The Standard Edition of the Complete Psychological Works of Sigmund Freud,* rev. and ed. James Strachey (London: The Hogarth Press and the Institute of Psycho-Analysis, 1957) , p. 31. Also see, with slight changes in translation, Sigmund Freud, "On the History of the Psycho-Analytic Movement" in *Early Papers and History of Psycho-Analytical Movement,* trans. Joan Riviere, vol. 1 of *Collected Papers,* The International Psycho-Analytical Library, ed. Ernest Jones, no. 7 (London: The Hogarth Press and the Institute of Psycho-Analysis, 1949) , p. 314. Incidentally, one of the auditors at Freud's lectures was William James, who was then fatally ill. He followed Freud's comments in German, which he knew well. Freud remarks about James's presence: "He was very friendly to us and I shall never forget his parting words, said with his arm around my shoulder: 'The future of psychology belongs to your work'—a remarkable saying when one reflects on his puritanical background." (Jones, 2:57)
4. A measure of the influence of psychology and psychoanalysis upon literature can be reasonably gauged from the following work: Norman Kiell, compiler and editor, *Psychoanalysis, Psychology and Literature: A Bibliography* (Madison: The University of Wisconsin Press, 1963) . There are over 4,400 titles here, appearing during the period 1900–1961, dealing with literary writings from a psychological point of view.

PSYCHOANALYTICALLY ORIENTED LITERARY CRITICISM
IN THE UNITED STATES

It is Hoffman's belief that during the twenties writers
who were drawn to Freud saw in his theories a means to
study the problem of sex. In the thirties, the literary study
of Freud was broader and more intelligent. Hoffman
makes an attempt to differentiate between the Freudian
practitioner and the literary man who uses Freud's meth-
ods in his work; he particularly singles out Edmund Wilson and Kenneth Burke as employing psychoanalysis in
critical judgment without being blinded to other literary
possibilities.

A second edition of Hoffman's work was published in
1957. The newer work also contains an appendix entitled
"Psychology and Literature" which was originally presented in lecture form at the English Institute in a sym-
posium called "Peripheries of Literature."[5] This newer
edition found Hoffman probing further into the dynamic
aspects of psychoanalytic literary criticism.

Between the publication years of Hoffman's two editions of *Freudianism and the Literary Mind,* Ernest Jones,
an English psychoanalyst and close disciple of Freud,
published his *Hamlet and Oedipus* in 1949. Based on an
examination of Sophocles' *Oedipus Rex* and Shakespeare's
Hamlet, the study concluded that Shakespeare's plot is in
essence a variation of the Greek tragedy by Sophocles.

In 1952 Ernst Kris edited *Psychoanalytic Explorations*

5. "Psychology and Literature" was also published in the Freud Cen-
tenary Number of *Literature and Psychology* 6 (1956) : 111–15, and in *The
Kenyon Review* 19 (Autumn 1957) : 605–19. More recently it has been published as "Literary Form and Psychic Tension," *Hidden Patterns: Studies
in Psychoanalytic Literary Criticism,* ed. Leonard and Eleanor Manheim
(New York: The Macmillan Company, 1966) , pp. 50–65.

in Art, which presented essays that combined years of research in art with clinical experience in psychoanalysis. Literary critics have found this volume a gold mine for further speculation and/or doubt. The same can also be said about *Art and Psychoanalysis,* published in 1957 and edited by William Phillips. The latter work also has the interesting subtitle of *Studies in the Application of Psychoanalytic Theory to the Creative Process.* Much is made in this work of the relationship between neurosis and art. While discussion still goes on among critics concerning the creator of a work of art, his product, and the creative process,[6] the psychoanalytically oriented literary critic is slowly emerging with a sure grasp of his field.

Of particular interest here is Louis Fraiberg's *Psychoanalysis and American Literary Criticism* published in 1960. He studies the influence of classical Freudian psychoanalysis on the American literary scene and employs a novel technique in doing so. First, Fraiberg considers the literature of Freud and three of his co-workers, Ernest Jones, Hanns Sachs, and Ernst Kris. Fraiberg is interested in psychoanalytic writings as they relate to art and more particularly to literature. Fraiberg is also interested here in communicating recent work in ego psychology. He considers the conscious part of the psyche important in the production of a work of art.

Second, Fraiberg presents six critics. These are Van Wyck Brooks, Joseph Wood Krutch, Ludwig Lewisohn, Edmund Wilson, Kenneth Burke, and Lionel Trilling. The first three of this group represent the early psychoanalytic critic of the twenties. Fraiberg is of the opinion that none of these three critics was able successfully to

---

6. This relationship from a psychoanalytic literary view has been studied by Edmund Bergler, *The Writer and Psychoanalysis* (Garden City, N.Y.: Doubleday & Company, Inc., 1950).

integrate literary criticism and psychoanalysis. Wilson, Burke, and Trilling, on the other hand, are more highly regarded by Fraiberg as literary critics, although they are seen as somewhat amiss in their understanding of psychoanalytic theory. Of the three, Fraiberg believes that Trilling is the most effective in his work as a critic. Fraiberg also points up the fact that Trilling particularly recognizes the importance of Freud's assertion of mind as being a poetry-making faculty.[7]

Another work to be mentioned here is *Hidden Patterns: Studies in Psychoanalytic Literary Criticism,* edited by Leonard and Eleanor Manheim and published in 1966. While essentially a compilation of previously published articles, this work tends to further refine psychoanalytic understanding of literature by stressing the function of good criticism. The editors write in the Introduction as follows:

> If the function of all good criticism is to send the reader back to the work itself, then we think that the selections made (out of a wealth of material, much of which we have, for various reasons, regretfully passed by) constitute very good criticism by any standard. We wish that we were still deep enough in the nineteenth century to be comfortable in addressing you by your proper title—gentle reader. Perhaps, though, you will not be so gentle when you have read these studies. You will be aroused, possibly fighting mad, possibly bemused with unsuspected possibilities and frightening depths. But we do not think you will be bored or indifferent. And in that spirit we present our book to you. (p. 13)

---

7. Interesting comments on Fraiberg's work can be found in Walter Sutton, *Modern American Criticism* (Englewood Cliffs, N.J.: Prentice-Hall, Inc., 1963) , pp. 243–49; also, in the following book review: Mark Kanzer, "Louis Fraiberg—*Psychoanalysis & American Literary Criticism,*" in *Literature and Psychology* 10 (Spring 1960) : 56–58.

PSYCHOANALYSIS AND POETRY

It is now clear that the psychoanalytically oriented criticism of American poetry developed as part of a similar criticism of American literature, and world literature in general. Our focus being on three American poets, we now turn to psychoanalysis and poetry in the United States.

Freud appreciated full well the value of the productions of literary figures in attempts to offer fresh insight into human behavior—hence his interest in the classics, Goethe, and poetry. We know, too, that Freud was interested in such figures as Moses, Leonardo da Vinci, Michelangelo, Shakespeare, and other creative personalities. One need only remind oneself of such terms as "Oedipus" and "Electra" as employed by Freud to see how the insights of poetic dramatists have become deeply integrated into Freudian theory.

In 1908 Freud wrote a paper entitled "The Relation of the Poet to Day-Dreaming."[8] In this paper he compares the imaginative writer with the day-dreamer and the work of the poet with the day-dream. In his presentation, Freud relates the concept of "phantasy" to the factor of time and wish-fulfillment. He explains his views as follows:

> One may say that a phantasy at one and the same moment hovers between three periods of time—the three periods of our ideation. The activity of phantasy in the

---

8. *Papers on Metapsychology; Papers on Applied Psycho-Analysis,* trans. Joan Riviere, vol. 4 of *Collected Papers,* The International Psycho-Analytical Library, ed. Ernest Jones, no. 10 (London: The Hogarth Press and the Institute of Psycho-Analysis, 1949) , pp. 173–83. Also, "The Relation of the Poet to Day-Dreaming" is retitled, with some changes in translation; see Sigmund Freud, "Creative Writers and Day-Dreaming" in *Jensen's 'Gradiva' and Other Works,* vol. 9 (1906–1908) of *The Standard Edition of the Complete Psychological Works of Sigmund Freud,* rev. and ed. James Strachey (London: The Hogarth Press and the Institute of Psycho-Analysis, 1959) , pp. 143–53.

mind is linked up with some current impression, occasioned by some event in the present, which had the power to rouse an intense desire. From there it wanders back to the memory of an early experience, generally belonging to infancy, in which this wish was fulfilled. Then it creates for itself a situation which is to emerge in the future, representing the fulfilment of the wish—this is the day-dream or phantasy, which now carries in it traces both of the occasion which engendered it and of some past memory. So past, present and future are threaded, as it were, on the string of the wish that runs through them all. (*Collected Papers*, 4: 177–78)

It is interesting to notice that in describing what is involved in the creation of poetry, Freud's explanation of the time factor is a fluid one. There is not only a relationship between fantasy and time here, but also between these and day-dreams and/or dreams. Freud writes:

I cannot pass over the relation or phantasies to dreams. Our nocturnal dreams are nothing but such phantasies, as we can make clear by interpreting them. Language, in its unrivalled wisdom, long ago decided the question of the essential nature of dreams by giving the name of 'day-dreams' to the airy creations of phantasy. If the meaning of our dreams usually remains obscure in spite of this clue, it is because of the circumstance that at night wishes of which we are ashamed also become active in us, wishes which we have to hide from ourselves, which were consequently repressed and pushed back into the unconscious. Such repressed wishes and their derivatives can therefore achieve expression only when almost completely disguised. When scientific work had succeeded in elucidating the distortion in dreams, it was no longer difficult to recognize that nocturnal dreams are fulfilments of desires in exactly the same way as day-dreams are—those phantasies with which we are all so familiar. (pp. 178–79)

Hence, according to the Freudian understanding of the poetic experience, something forbidden is involved in the art of writing poetry. While the concern in this study is not with the art of creativity, it seems, in light of the above, that critics employing psychoanalytic knowledge in explaining poetry have apparently come close to the sources of creativity.

Writing about creativity and the poet, Jung sees the poet's life as being unimportant in explaining his work: ". . . the personal life of the poet cannot be held essential to his art. . . . His personal career may be inevitable and interesting, but it does not explain the poet."[9] What Jung believes, insofar as the poet's work is concerned, is that the poem touches something in man that deals with the problem of human existence, not particularly from a personal idiosyncratic point of view. Furthermore, from a psychoanalytic frame of reference, Jung says: "A great work of art is like a dream; for all its apparent obviousness it does not explain itself and is never unequivocal" (p. 171).

It appears then that both Freud and Jung, while approaching poetry by way of dream interpretation, offer no final assurance as to what constitutes a psychoanalytic interpretation of poetry.

In April 1912 an American journal, devoted primarily to articles pertaining to psychology, contained a discussion of unusual interest for that time. The *Journal of Abnormal Psychology* included an article essentially of literary import but having psychological overtones.[10] Stanley Burnshaw, writing the Foreword to a reprint of a book by the author of the article, stated:

---

9. *Modern Man in Search of a Soul,* trans. W. S. Dell and Cary F. Baynes (New York: Harcourt, Brace & World, Inc., 1933) , p. 172.
10. Frederick C. Prescott, "Poetry and Dreams," *Journal of Abnormal Psychology* 7 (April 1912) : 17–46, 104–43.

Its author, Frederick C. Prescott, was not a psychologist but a teacher of English at Cornell, a forty-year-old
Kansan who had studied and taught at Harvard. "Poetry
and Dreams" was followed by a second installment, and
then the two were generally ignored, even when issued
separately in 1912 and 1919. By the year following the
last publication, however, the original seventy pages
had become a full-length study of the operation of the
poet's mind, a subject described by its author as "lying
halfway between psychology and literature."[11]

In Prescott we observe probably the first incursion of
a respectable American literary person into formal psychological territory on the American scene, dealing with the
topic of poetry.

Burnshaw, a poet in his own right and himself a former
student of Prescott, also observes the following:

When *The Poetic Mind* appeared in 1922, reviewers
examined it with care but little relish, and its existence
could hardly have been detected throughout the suc-
ceeding twenty years. But then rediscovery set in. Critics
began to refer to Prescott as a pioneer and to his book
as having been ahead of its time. Today *The Poetic
Mind* is "classified"—as "one of the first notable efforts
to relate Freudian theory to a theory of poetry" (Herbert J. Muller) or "the first careful adaptation of Freudian theory to literature" (William Van O'Connor).
(Prescott, p. v)

If we keep in mind Freud's coming to the United States
in December 1909 and the date of the publication of Prescott's article in the *Journal of Abnormal Psychology* in
April 1912, we see that a relatively short time ensued between Freud's visit and the above-stated expression about

11. Foreword to Frederick C. Prescott, *The Poetic Mind* (Ithaca: Cornell University Press, 1959; 1st ed., New York: The Macmillan Company,
1922), p. v.

dynamic psychology and poetry in an American publication. However, a fuller treatment of such expression was
given in 1922 in *The Poetic Mind.* This meant that in a
period of approximately thirteen years a full-length work
dealing with some aspects of Freudian psychoanalysis and
poetry appeared on the American scene.

A considered evaluation of Prescott's presentation in his
1912 articles and *The Poetic Mind* raises many questions
concerning the observations of Muller, Van O'Connor, and
Burnshaw. Prescott seems to accept Freud's views of the
unconscious with some Jungian deviation, as is suggested
in the following:

> A man chooses his mate not consciously and voluntarily,
> but in exactly the opposite way; he finds himself in love.
> And this perhaps because the choice is not so much an
> individual matter, as one which concerns the race as
> a whole, which cannot be left to individual volition.
> The deeper choice is the wiser. And in general the
> imaginings of the unconscious mind will represent a
> deeper wisdom and morality. The subject is much too
> large to be treated in a paragraph; but I think careful
> consideration might show that the responsibility of the
> individual to society or to morality in conscious thought
> and action is one thing, and the responsibility in vision-
> ary unconscious thought quite another; and that though
> the dreamer is freed from social obligation in a narrow
> sense, he is brought into relation with the mind of the
> race in a larger way and thus subjected to a more pro-
> found control. (*The Poetic Mind,* pp. 116–17) [12]

12. It is interesting to compare this quotation from Prescott with that
of Jung. In speaking of the collective unconscious, Jung writes: "These
are the mythological associations—those motives and images which can
spring anew in every age and clime, without historical tradition or
migration. I term these contents the *collective unconscious.* Just as
conscious contents are engaged in a definite activity, the unconscious contents—so experience teaches us—are similarly active. Just as certain results
or products proceed from conscious psychic activity, there are also products of unconscious activity, as for instance dreams and phantasies." C. G.
Jung, *Psychological Types,* trans. H. Godwin Baynes (London: Routledge

In the above statement we have one of the main differences between Freud and Jung on the theory of the unconscious. The latter believes in an unconscious that contains elements of "racial memories." Be that as it may, Prescott not only follows Freud's view of the unconscious, with the above exception, but he also holds fast to Freud's concept of dream interpretation when dealing with the actual operations of poetic thought.[13]

While Prescott counted heavily on Freud, he also was dependent for some of his thinking on the ideas advanced by the Reverend John Keble. "Indeed if *The Poetic Mind* was noteworthy for relating Freud to literature, it was even more remarkable for rescuing and emphasizing the radical ideas that Keble had ventured eighteen years before the birth of Freud" (Burnshaw, p. vi). In this same context, Burnshaw points out some salient facts about Keble, an Anglican clergyman who was responsible for setting off the Oxford movement with his St. Mary's sermon of 1883. Keble believed that literature was a form of disguised wish-fulfillment, that poetry provided a catharsis that saved men from becoming mad, and that the writer was concerned with unconscious material of an autobiographical nature.

While Prescott utilized all this information in the development of his interest in the relation of poetry to psychoanalysis, he never maintained a strict Freudian view. He does, however, concern himself with two major psychoanalytic aspects of poetry. These are: (1) unconscious determinants of poetic inspiration, such as are found in dreams, and (2) the phenomenon of dream life and its

---

& Kegan Paul Ltd., 1953), p. 616. It is also interesting to point out in passing that Prescott dealt with poetry and myth more extensively in a later work, *Poetry and Myth* (New York: The Macmillan Company, 1927).

13. See especially Chap. 8, "The Desires and Emotions in Poetry," *The Poetic Mind*, pp. 122–38.

relationship to the phenomenon of poetic expression.[14]

Essentially then we may draw an inference that the unconscious and dream phenomena are basic tools in understanding, criticizing, and evaluating the field of poetry from a psychoanalytic frame of reference. Incidentally, these psychoanalytic tools are employed singly and/or together, whether the focal point of interest is the work itself or the creator, regardless of one's psychoanalytic allegiance.[15]

And literary critics of the 1920s were not particularly loyal to any one school of psychology. They took a great deal from Freud, and later on from Jung; there were also other schools of psychology that affected their outlook.[16] But since our concern is primarily with the psychoanalytically oriented criticism of poetry, a discussion of critics employing other schools of psychology is not pertinent here.

Ludwig Lewisohn's *Expression in America* was published in 1932 and reissued in 1939 under a new title— *The Story of American Literature.*[17] He was of the belief

---

14. Frederick J. Hoffman also notes this concern of Prescott in *Freudianism and the Literary Mind,* 2d ed. (Baton Rouge: Louisiana State University Press, 1957), p. 99. We are reminded in a footnote on the same page: "Dr. Brill said that he and Prescott had conferred frequently about the latter's book, checking it with Freudian theory, and that Prescott had in turn helped Brill with his translations. Interview of December, 1942."

15. Lest there be unnecessary confusion at this point, it is well to keep in mind Hoffman's admonition: "A study of poets need not distort the understanding of their poetry. The greatest defect of this kind of biographical analysis lies essentially in its ignoring the work or merely using it as accessory evidence for the analysis of the writer." (p. 98)

16. An excellent summary of the salient points of literary criticism including psychology and psychoanalysis can be found in Alex Preminger, ed., *Encyclopedia of Poetry and Poetics* (Princeton: Princeton University Press, 1965), pp. 158–74.

17. Lewisohn combines the psychoanalytic interest of the twenties and the sociological interest of the thirties in this work. Individual psyche and social environment are both stressed as important factors of the human condition. He deals among other literary personalities with Hawthorne, Melville, Poe, Whitman, Stephen Crane, Frank Norris, Henry James, D. H. Lawrence, and Theodore Dreiser.

that the future rested with such figures as E. A. Robinson,
William Ellery Leonard, and Vachel Lindsay. He could
not say much for the newer poetry of Pound, Eliot, Williams, and Cummings.

Sutton summarizes Lewisohn's work as follows:

> Such eccentricity of judgment is common in Lewi-
> sohn's work. His simplified Freudian ideas are often rele-
> vant to the lives of American writers, but he fails to use
> them as tools of literary criticism. *Expression in Amer-
> ica* is essentially a study of culture rather than of liter-
> ature. In combining an interest in psychoanalysis and
> the romantic tradition, it is typical of early psychologi-
> cal criticism. Many critics, unable to accept the full
> implications of Freud's thought, attempted the difficult
> task of reconciling it with revelation theories and similar
> romantic ideas. In later years, critics thus inclined
> identified themselves with Jungian myth criticism, while
> Freudian criticism developed along lines more consistent
> with psychoanalytical principles. (*Modern American
> Criticism*, p. 25)

In 1939, Kenneth Burke wrote directly of Freud and
poetry.[18] While appreciating Freud's contribution to the
study of literature and poetry, Burke places his emphasis
upon communication. Admitting that the act of the poet
and that of the neurotic are primarily symbolic acts, he
believes the key to literary analysis is communication
rather than wish-fulfillment. Hence, Burke believes that
Freudian theory can be revised and still be most effective
in criticism of poetry. Burke writes:

> But such revisions would by no means be anti-Freud-
> ian. They would be the kind of extensions required by

18. "Freud—and the Analysis of Poetry," *American Journal of Sociology*
45 (1939): 391–417; reprinted in *Psychoanalysis and Literature,* ed. Hendrik M. Ruitenbeek (New York: E. P. Dutton & Co., Inc., 1964), pp.
114–41. The latter source is used here.

reason of the fact that the symbolic act of art, whatever its analogies with the symbolic act of neurosis, also has important divergencies from the symbolic act of neurosis. They would be extensions designed to take into account the full play of communicative and realistic ingredients that comprise so large an aspect of poetic structure. (p. 137)

It is important to note here that Kenneth Burke as a literary critic is interested in psychoanalysis, particularly if it can help in better communication. The psychoanalytic approach to poetry, while not denying the importance of better communication, emphasizes personality aspects of the poet and/or his work.[19] Burke, as one can see, is arguing for a more comprehensive utility of psychoanalytic understanding when it comes to poetry.

This survey of psychoanalysis and poetry has provided a framework for the more detailed study of the psychoanalytically oriented criticism of Poe, Whitman, and Aiken.

---

19. A good example here in addition to the works of Freud already cited is A. A. Brill, "Poetry as an Oral Outlet," *The Psychoanalytic Review* 18 (October 1931): 357–78. Brill seeks proof for his views in oral outlets "among the neurotic, the psychotic, the child, and the primitive."

2
Edgar Allan Poe

ATTEMPTS TO STUDY POE PSYCHOANALYTICALLY

Edgar Allan Poe's life (1809–1849) was so psychologically complicated that psychoanalytically oriented writers can easily find in it gold mines of information for their theories. Poe's writing includes, among other topics, such themes as love, horror, anxiety, fantasy, and strange conditions of the mind. His material, therefore, is also a "natural" for psychological theories that are concerned with personality aberrations.[1] His life is extremely enticing in this direction and has led critic Vincent Buranelli to make the following comment:

> Edgar Allan Poe is the most complex personality in the entire gallery of American authors. No one else fuses, as he does, such discordant psychological attributes, or offers to the world an appearance so various. No one else stands at the center of a mystery so profound. Hawthorne, Melville and Faulkner are, by comparison with Poe, easy enough to classify, while Edwards, Cooper and

1. One of the most balanced and best-written biographies of Poe is Arthur Hobson Quinn's *Edgar Allan Poe: A Critical Biography* (New York: D. Appleton-Century Company, Inc., 1941). Another work of interest here is Hervey Allen, *Israfel: The Life and Times of Edgar Allan Poe* (New York: Farrar & Rinehart, Inc., 1934). For comprehensive bibliographical information on Poe, see Jay B. Hubbell, "Poe," in *Eight American Authors: A Review of Research and Criticism,* ed. Floyd Stovall (New York: W. W. Norton & Company, Inc., 1963), pp. 1–46.

Hemingway emerge with crystal clarity. Poe resists easy interpretation and broad generalization. Any plausible analysis of his work, like any authentic story of his life, must begin with this primary and essential truth.[2]

Even the simplest of personalities contain complexity that is often misunderstood. And Poe's was no simple personality. With excellent understanding of the personality makeup of an artist like Poe, Buranelli also reminds us:

> It is false to call him little more than an artist of nightmares, hallucinations, insane crimes and weird beauties, little more than an intuitive poetic genius dabbling in pretentious logic when he is not lost in the black forest of pathological psychology. Nor is he a frigid allegorist living in an ivory tower safely away from the contamination of the world. Poe is a dreamer (in the widest sense of the term), and that is where an analytical study may properly begin; but it must not end until it has accounted for Poe the rationalist, the scientist, the hoaxer, the humorist, and the literary and social critic. (p. 19)

The fact that Poe's poetic genius was tied to a distorted personal life was bound to affect his feeling and thinking. These ideas and emotions in turn were naturally reflected in his work. But Philip Lindsay exhibits the real dangers of psychoanalytically oriented criticism when he shifts the focus from the work of art to the case history in a passage like the following:

> Son of shiftless parents and at an early age fatherless and motherless, Edgar Poe was born to live in nightmare. His life, almost from birth, might well have been his own creation, following a pattern similar to one of

---

2. *Edgar Allan Poe* (New York: Twayne Publishers, Inc., 1961), p. 17. A further consideration of the psyche of Poe can be found in Killis Campbell, *The Mind of Poe and Other Studies* (Cambridge: Harvard University Press, 1933).

his tales, macabre and frenzied and ending on a note of
pointless tragedy. The story, *William Wilson,* was largely
autobiographical, not only in external details, but in its
emotional content. Here, Poe opened his heart and con-
fessed that his own pitiless destroyer was himself. Most
men, were they honest, might make a similar confes-
sion. Yet with Poe this was not entirely true. He might
have destroyed himself but the seeds of that destruction
were germinated in childhood. Always haunting him
was the thought of death in love, of the death of his
mother, then of the death of a woman he loved, then of
the death of his foster-mother, and finally of his wife.
These four he loved died as though his kiss were lethal.
In the grave, surrendered to the conqueror worm, their
once quick flesh rotted, and his desires turned naturally
from life towards death. Death, the enemy, became the
loved one, and he relished more the thought of dissolution than the living body he clasped, feeling always the
skull beneath the hair he touched, the small bones mov-
ing in the hand he clasped, and the teeth felt under a
kiss.[3]

Poe's strange life has been considered in several ways.
One of the attempts as early as 1920 to study Poe as an
aberrant personality was that made by Lorine Pruette.[4] In
addition to relating, along psychoanalytic lines, some of
Poe's poetry to some of the early determinants of Poe's
life, Pruette is also concerned with the "individual psychology" of Alfred Adler. "The organic inferiority of both
lungs and mind, if we follow the theories of Adler, de-
manded compensation, which the youth found in drawing
and in writing stories and poems" (Pruette, p. 375).[5] Poe's

3. *The Haunted Man: A Portrait of Edgar Allan Poe* (London: Hutch-
inson & Co. Ltd., 1953), p. 11.
4. "A Psycho-Analytical Study of Edgar Allan Poe," *The American
Journal of Psychology* 31 (October 1920): 370–402.
5. For information on Adler's views see Alfred Adler, *The Practice and
Theory of Individual Psychology,* trans. P. Radin (London: K. Paul,
Trench, Trubner & Co., Ltd., 1946); Alfred Adler, *What Life Should
Mean to You,* ed. Alan Porter (Boston: Little, Brown and Company, 1931);

"will to power," Pruette believes, "would brook no supe-rior, nor even equal, in either physical or mental pursuits, and it was this intolerance of the claims of mediocrity which brought upon him in later life the enmity of much of the literary world" (p. 375) . Pruette also points out that Poe was of the belief "that his absolutely unswerving devo-tion to truth was responsible for his scathing criticisms" (p. 375) . But Poe's own "devotion to truth" was still tied to a personality that was in a constant state of anxiety and unrest.[6] And in her monumental psychoanalytical study of Poe, Marie Bonaparte[7] emphasizes that Poe's achievement could primarily be understood in terms of the pathological trends in Poe's life. Freud made a special point of this when in the Foreword to Bonaparte's work, he wrote: "Thanks to her interpretative effort, we now realize how many of the characteristics of Poe's works were condi-tioned by his personality, and can see how that personality derived from intense emotional fixations and painful in-fantile experiences."[8]

Heinz L. Ansbacher and Rowena R. Ansbacher, eds., *The Individual Psychology of Alfred Adler* (New York: Basic Books, Inc., 1956) ; and Kurt A. Adler and Danica Deutsch, eds., *Essays in Individual Psychology: Contemporary Application of Alfred Adler's Theories* (New York: Grove Press, Inc., 1959) .

6. It is also interesting to note the following remarks of Pruette: "With woman poets, Poe was seldom, almost never, critical. His desire for superiority seemed with women to take an entirely different form. He had the characteristic over-valuation of the opposite sex which, accord-ing to Adler, is invariably connected with the neurotic constitution." (p. 375)

7. *The Life and Works of Edgar Allan Poe: A Psycho-Analytic In-terpretation*, trans. John Rodker (London: Imago Publishing Co. Ltd., 1949) .

8. Freud also went on to state in the Foreword that while investiga-tions such as Bonaparte's may not explain genius, underlying factors are revealed about phenomena that awaken the creative aspects of genius and the subject-matter that people of this calibre are destined to choose (p. xi) . Interestingly enough, it should be quite evident by now that state-ments about Poe and/or his work from a depth psychology point of view are often quite inconclusive. In addition to the above comments, Poe's life has been studied in the present century by the neurologist Dr. John W. Robertson, who spoke of Poe in terms of a "bad heredity," and by

PSYCHOANALYTICALLY ORIENTED CRITICISM OF
SELECTED POE POETRY

To enlarge our scope of understanding of the psycho-analytically oriented criticism of selected Poe poetry, an important point must be kept in mind. Poe's poetic endeavors were based on a definite belief that he had of poetry. He states his rationale as follows:

> A poem, in my opinion, is opposed to a work of science by having, for its *immediate* object, pleasure, not truth; to romance, by having for its object an *indefinite* instead of a *definite* pleasure, being a poem only so far as this object is attained; romance presenting perceptible images with definite, poetry with *in*definite sensations, to which end music is an *essential,* since the comprehension of sweet sound is our most indefinite conception. Music, when combined with a pleasurable idea, is poetry; music without the idea is simply music; the idea without the music is prose from its very definitiveness.[9]

Joseph Wood Krutch, who thought of Poe as suffering from a "mother" fixation and hence created an abnormal world in order to compensate for sexual impotency. See John W. Robertson, *Edgar A. Poe* (San Francisco: B. Brough, 1921) , and Joseph Wood Krutch, *Edgar Allan Poe: A Study in Genius* (New York: Russell & Russell, Inc., 1965) . Also, for an interesting and comprehensive article providing historical information about attempts to understand Poe's life psychologically, see the following: Philip Young, "The Earlier Psychologists and Poe," *American Literature* 22 (January 1951) : 442–54.

9. "Letter to B———," *Selected Writings of Edgar Allan Poe,* ed. Edward H. Davidson (Boston: Houghton Mifflin Company, 1956) , pp. 414–15. Pleasure and a high sense of beauty: these were two important aspects of Poe's criticism regarding all genres. But in Freudian psychoanalytic terms, pleasure and beauty have special meanings. Basic to an understanding of Freud's psychology is the concept of pleasure and unpleasure. In brief, Freud believes that when there is a feeling on the part of the individual's ego that tensions are being raised, one is encountering unpleasure, while the lowering or relaxation of tensions or absence of pressures is felt as pleasure. Beauty is thought of as closely related to the very experience of civilization; that is, Freud believes that the lack of beauty is something civilization will not tolerate. After speaking of happiness and love, Freud says: "We may go on from here to consider the interesting case in which happiness in life is predominantly sought in the

So strongly was the above view a guiding belief in all of Poe's work that Norman Foerster remarked: "This was Poe's artistic creed, exemplified in nearly all that he wrote: in his poetry, his tales, his essays on literary theory, and his criticism of literature—on nearly every page of his sixteen volumes."[10]

Poe's definition of poetry has been viewed by Pruette in a broader psychoanalytic sense as follows:

> The poems of Poe are songs of sorrow: beauty is in them, most often dead beauty, love is there, most often the love of those who are dead to him, and madness is there, as if the expression of the prophetic powers of his unconscious. Often enough, in moments of extreme depression, under the influence of drugs or in the temporary insanity induced by the use of stimulants, must he himself have felt those "evil things, in robes of sorrow," which "assailed the monarch's high estate." ("A Psycho-Analytical Study of Edgar Allan Poe," p. 384)

Beauty and pleasure often appear together in dreams.[11]

---

enjoyment of beauty, wherever beauty presents itself to our senses and our judgement—the beauty of human forms and gestures, of natural objects and landscapes and of artistic and even scientific creations. This aesthetic attitude to the goal of life offers little protection against the threat of suffering, but it can compensate for a great deal. The enjoyment of beauty has a peculiar, mildly intoxicating quality of feeling. Beauty has no obvious use; nor is there any clear cultural necessity for it. Yet civilization could not do without it." See Sigmund Freud, *Civilization and Its Discontents,* ed. and trans. by James Strachey (New York: W. W. Norton & Co., Inc., 1961) , pp. 29–30.

10. *American Criticism: A Study in Literary Theory from Poe to the Present* (New York: Russell & Russell, Inc., 1962) , p. 7. Foerster has a keen perception about Poe's view of pleasure and beauty. He develops these other themes with much wisdom in the section of the work entitled "Poe," pp. 1–51. It is also important here to point out that one American critic in particular has disputed Poe's ability as a writer and has also questioned Poe's concepts, especially as regards "beauty" and "pleasure." See Yvor Winters, "Edgar Allan Poe: A Crisis in the History of American Obscurantism," *Maule's Curse: Seven Studies in the History of American Obscurantism* (Norfolk, Conn.: New Directions, 1938) , pp. 93–122.

11. For those interested in the Freudian theory of dreams, see "The

Frequently these are intertwined with a desire for love fulfillment, and in real life give an impression of happiness, which is often referred to as a dream. That Poe has captured this feeling is indicated in the last eight lines of his poem entitled "Dreams":[12]

> I have been happy, tho' but in a dream.
> I have been happy—and I love the theme:
> Dreams! in their vivid colouring of life
> As in that fleeting, shadowy, misty strife
> Of semblance with reality which brings
> To the delirious eye, more lovely things
> Of Paradise and Love—and all our own!
> Than young Hope in his sunniest hour hath known.[13]

Interpretation of Dreams," in *The Basic Writings of Sigmund Freud,* trans. and ed. A. A. Brill (New York: Random House, Inc., 1938), pp. 181–549. Also refer to the following: Sigmund Freud, *The Interpretation of Dreams* (1), vol. 4 (1900) of *The Standard Edition of the Complete Psychological Works of Sigmund Freud,* rev. and ed. James Strachey (London: The Hogarth Press and the Institute of Psycho-Analysis, 1953); and Sigmund Freud, *The Interpretation of Dreams* (11) and *On Dreams,* vol. 5 (1900–1901) of *The Standard Edition of the Complete Psychological Works of Sigmund Freud,* rev. and ed. James Strachey (London: The Hogarth Press and the Institute of Psycho-Analysis, 1953). For a discussion of the Jungian theory of dream interpretation, refer to comments in the following works: C. G. Jung, *The Archetypes and the Collective Unconscious,* in *Collected Works of C. G. Jung,* Bollingen Series 20, ed. Herbert Read, Michael Fordham, and Gerhard Adler. Gerhard Adler, vol. 9, trans. R. F. C. Hull (New York: Pantheon Books, 1959), part 1; *The Development of Personality,* in *Collected Works,* vol. 17, trans. by R. F. C. Hull (New York: Pantheon Books, 1954); *Symbols of Transformation,* in *Collected Works,* vol. 5, trans. R. F. C. Hull (New York: Pantheon Books, 1956); and *The Psychogenesis of Mental Disease,* in *Collected Works,* vol. 3, trans. R. F. C. Hull (New York: Pantheon Books, 1960). For those interested in an Adlerian point of view on dream interpretation, see: Alfred Adler, "Dreams," *What Life Should Mean to You,* ed. Alan Porter (Boston: Little, Brown and Company, 1931), pp. 93–119; also, see references to dreams in the following: Alfred Adler, *The Practice and Theory of Individual Psychology,* trans. P. Radin (London: K. Paul, Trench, Trubner & Co., Ltd., 1946); Heinz L. Ansbacher and Rowena R. Ansbacher, eds., *The Individual Psychology of Alfred Adler* (New York: Basic Books, Inc., 1956).

12. Floyd Stovall, ed., *The Poems of Edgar Allan Poe* (Charlottesville: The University Press of Virginia, 1965), pp. 13–14. Unless otherwise noted, all of the poems discussed herein are from this work.

13. This poem, "Dreams," was originally part of the volume *Tamerlane and Other Poems* (1827). Marie Bonaparte believes that this work

These lines were published when Poe was still a relatively young man. It appears that he felt deeply apart from humanity at this time. Joseph Wood Krutch has stated:

> It was natural that a young man who felt, as Poe did, desperately isolated from the rest of mankind should find his model in the most popular poet of melodramatic isolation and so, though traces of Keats, Shelley, and Coleridge have been found in him, the dominant influence is obviously Byronic.[14]

Based on another poem, entitled "A Dream," the critics give us further insights into Poe's past hopes and his present situation as well as a contrast between the world of reality and the world of fancy, all closely related to dreams, fantasies, day-dreams, and wish-fulfillments.[15]

---

contained poems that were "all melancholy in cast." She believes this may be partially owing to the romantic spirit of the age. (*The Life and Works of Edgar Allan Poe: A Psycho-Analytic Interpretation,* p. 37)

14. *Edgar Allan Poe: A Study in Genius,* p. 65. This same critic also develops the concept of Poe's wishes and dreams as being caused to a large extent by "ferocious and reckless egotism." See Joseph Wood Krutch, "The Strange Case of Poe," *The American Mercury* 6 (November 1925) : 349–56. Also see Joseph Wood Krutch, "Genius and Neuroticism" in *And Even If You Do* (New York: William Morrow & Company, Inc., 1967) , pp. 145–52. And since dreams are to Freud disguised wish-fulfillments, and since they are often related to childhood's state of omnipotence and a feeling of happiness, there is a coming together in these lines of the past and present. In Freudian psychoanalytic theory the time factor of past and present are inextricably bound up with the future insofar as the day-dream wish is concerned. This idea is given fuller treatment in the following work: Sigmund Freud, "The Relation of the Poet to Day-Dreaming," *Collected Papers,* ed. Ernest Jones (London: The Hogarth Press and the Institute of Psycho-Analysis, 1949) , 4: 173–83.

Incidentally, the concept of happiness as expressed in the above poem "Dreams" does not blind Poe to stark reality. For at the base of this poem is a wish-fulfillment. And in light of modern psychoanalytic theory, I suggest that Poe reveals a profound awareness of dreams without being a trained practitioner.

15. Of interest here too is the fact that Walt Whitman relates a dream and concludes that the lurid figure appearing in the dream might be Edgar Allan Poe. Whitman was of the belief that all of Poe's poems were "lurid dreams." See F. O. Matthiessen, *American Renaissance* (New York: Oxford University Press, Inc., 1941) , p. 541. Matthiessen makes a point of reminding readers that Whitman's comment about Poe "defines by implication his own aims." (p. 540)

A Dream

In visions of the dark night
    I have dreamed of joy departed—
But a waking dream of life and light
    Hath left me broken-hearted.

Ah! what is not a dream by day
    To him whose eyes are cast
On things around him with a ray
    Turned back upon the past?

That holy dream—that holy dream,
    While all the world were chiding,
Hath cheered me as a lovely beam
    A lonely spirit guiding.

What though that light, thro' storm and night,
    So trembled from afar—
What could there be more purely bright
    In Truth's day-star?

(Stovall, p. 21)

In commenting on the above poem, Pruette points out that in "A Dream" one can see Poe in the midst of the experience of "the contrast between what he has and what he has wanted, between the real and the ideal world of fancy" (p. 382). Also, the poem uses such images as "the dark night," "the past," "holy dream," "lonely spirit," and concludes with a resounding statement. The last stanza, while taking into account the reality of the dark side of life, ends in the form of a question expressing a wish. The word "Truth's" in the last line points up something special here. Truth and science are closely related. Both have a way of shaking men out of their dreams. Both have a way of making dreams a reality if the dreams are based on verifiable assumptions.[16] Hence, it is an easy step to go

---

16. In writing of science and truth as contrasted with religious claims, Freud wrote: "Scientific thought is, in its essence, no different from the normal process of thinking, which we all, believers and unbelievers, alike,

from this "A Dream" to Poe's "Sonnet—To Science." Writing as though he were thoroughly acquainted with psychoanalytical theory, Poe's "Sonnet—To Science" offers some keen insights into reality and dreams.

Sonnet—To Science

Science! true daughter of Old Time thou art!
　　Who alterest all things with thy peering eyes.
Why preyest thou thus upon the poet's heart,
　　Vulture, whose wings are dull realities?
How should he love thee? or how deem thee wise,
　　Who wouldst not leave him in his wandering
To seek for treasure in the jewelled skies,
　　Albeit he soared with an undaunted wing?
Hast thou not dragged Diana from her car?
　　And driven the Hamadryad from the wood
To seek a shelter in some happier star?
　　Hast thou not torn the Naiad from her flood,
The Elfin from the green grass, and from me
　　The summer dream beneath the tamarind tree?

(Stovall, p. 24)

In asking many questions of science, Poe is actually revealing its power, especially in the use of the word "vulture" in the fourth line of the above poem. Poe is reminding science that she has forced the seer, the poet,

make use of when we are going about our business in everyday life. It has merely taken a special form in certain respects: it extends its interest to things which have no immediate obvious utility, it endeavours to eliminate personal factors and emotional influences, it carefully examines the trustworthiness of the sense perceptions on which it bases its conclusions, it provides itself with new perceptions which are not obtainable by everyday means, and isolates the determinants of these new experiences by purposely varied experimentation. Its aim is to arrive at correspondence with reality, that is to say with what exists outside us and independently of us, and, as experience has taught us, is decisive for the fulfilment or frustration of our desires. This correspondence with the real external world we call truth. It is the aim of scientific work, even when the practical value of that work does not interest us." See Sigmund Freud, *New Introductory Lectures on Psycho-Analysis*, trans. W. J. H. Sprott (New York: W. W. Norton and Company, Inc., 1933), pp. 232–33.

to come back to reality, and that the Elysian fields of childhood are only dreams. Here we have Freud's concepts of the reality and pleasure principles further emphasized.[17] Dreams may be forms of wish fulfillments, but science with its emphasis on reality and truth forces one to look at himself, into himself, and at the world around him with great honesty. He is saying all this while voicing the objection of the romanticist "that the scientific attitude reduces everything to the most prosaic reality."[18]

Bonaparte argues that Poe looks upon science as a hated father. She also makes it a point to stress the idea that "true daughter of Old Time" in the first line is

the appanage of Time, thus being identified, in accordance with the process of the unconscious—which in this case troubles itself little about sex—with Time and so the "father." This was another reason why Poe hated science and would hate it, as bitterly, all his life. (*The Life and Works of Edgar Allan Poe: A Psycho-Analytic Interpretation*, p. 56)

In light of Bonaparte's comments, one might be tempted to forget that beauty and truth were of vital concern to Poe. He writes about this while discussing "The Raven," and touches upon beauty and truth in poetry:

When, indeed, men speak of Beauty, they mean, precisely, not a quality, as is supposed, but an effect—they refer, in short, just to that intense and pure elevation of

17. In essence, the reality principle as propounded by Freud holds that the mature ego can postpone the need for immediate gratification, can learn to endure a degree of frustration, and pain, and can renounce certain sources of satisfaction for a greater gain at a later time. The pleasure-principle is the opposite, where the psychical activity of the individual is bent on immediate gratification. See Sigmund Freud, *A General Introduction to Psychoanalysis*, trans. by Joan Riviere (Garden City, N.Y.: Garden City Publishing Company, Inc., 1943), pp. 311–12.

18. Harry Levin, *The Power of Blackness* (New York: Alfred A. Knopf, Inc., 1958), p. 137.

soul—not of intellect, or of heart—upon which I have
commented, and which is experienced in consequence
of contemplating the "beautiful." Now I designate
Beauty as the province of the poem, merely because it
is an obvious rule of Art that effects should be made to
spring from direct causes—that objects should be attained through means best adapted for their attain-
ment—no one as yet having been weak enough to deny
that the peculiar elevation alluded to is *most readily*
attained in the poem. Now the object Truth, or the
satisfaction of the intellect, and the object Passion, or
the excitement of the heart, are, although attainable to
a certain extent in poetry, far more readily attainable
in prose. Truth, in fact, demands a precision, and passion, a *homeliness* (the truly passionate will compre-
hend me), which are absolutely antagonistic to that
Beauty which, I maintain, is the excitement, or pleasur-
able elevation of the soul.[19]

Poe goes on to emphasize, in the same text, that passion
and truth may be profitably introduced into poetry. For
these two phenomena, passion and truth, may be employed
when properly used as means of making the poem itself a
more effective work of art and beauty.

Beauty, truth, and science also demand a disciplined
appreciation. The reality of life, the remembrance of the
beautiful, the realization that nature is oblivious to our
desires require a high level degree of understanding. In
the poem "A Dream Within a Dream" the last stanza reads
as follows:

> I stand amid the roar
> Of a surf-tormented shore,
> And I hold within my hand
> Grains of the golden sand—

---

19. "The Philosophy of Composition," in *The Complete Poems and
Stories of Edgar Allan Poe, With Selections from His Critical Writings,*
ed. Arthur Hobson Quinn and Edward H. O'Neill (New York: Alfred A.
Knopf, Inc., 1951), 2: 980–81.

How few! yet how they creep
Through my fingers to the deep,
While I weep—while I weep!
O God! can I not grasp
Them with a tighter clasp?
O God! can I not save
One from the pitiless wave?
Is all that we see or seem
But a dream within a dream?
                    (Stovall, p. 18)

The idea that truth, reality, and a moment of beauty
are all ephemeral forms is put in the form of a question
about a dream within a dream.[20] And according to Pruette,
"In 'A Dream Within a Dream' we find rebellion against
the disappointments of life" ("A Psycho-Analytical Study
of Edgar Allan Poe," p. 382). Always then we are confronted in Poe's poetry with questions of truth, beauty,
pleasure, reality, and dream, the very essentials of one's

---

20. This idea of "dream within a dream" has special meaning in
Freudian theory and psychoanalytic criticism, as is indicated in the following: "As for the judgment which is often expressed during a dream:
'Of course, it is only a dream,' and the psychic force to which it may be
ascribed, I shall discuss these questions later on. For the present I will
merely say that they are intended to depreciate the importance of what is
being dreamed. The interesting problem allied to this, as to what is
meant if a certain content in the dream is characterized in the dream
itself as having been 'dreamed'—the riddle of a 'dream within a dream'—
has been solved in a similar sense by W. Stekel, by the analysis of some
convincing examples. Here again the part of the dream 'dreamed' is to be
depreciated in value and robbed of its reality; that which the dreamer
continues to dream after waking from the 'dream within a dream' is what
the dream-wish desires to put in place of the obliterated reality. It may
therefore be assumed that the part 'dreamed' contains the representation
of the reality, the real memory, while, on the other hand, the continued
dream contains the representation of what the dreamer merely wishes.
The inclusion of a certain content in 'a dream within a dream' is therefore equivalent to the wish that what has been characterized as a dream
had never occurred. In other words: when a particular incident is repre-
sented by the dream-work in a 'dream,' it signifies the strongest confirma-
tion of the reality of this incident, the most emphatic *affirmation* of it.
The dream-work utilizes the dream itself as a form of repudiation, and
thereby confirms the theory that a dream is a wish-fulfillment." See Sigmund Freud, "The Interpretation of Dreams," *Basic Writings,* p. 360.

involvement with living and the core of modern depth psychology.

Modern depth psychologists believe that part of a creative person's contribution in his work is often a child-like quality of appreciation and awe; one can easily find these qualities in the poems of Poe, particularly in those that are intended to evoke a sadness or a yearning for the past or faraway places. The opening stanza of Part I of the poem "Al Aaraaf" certainly exemplifies this:

> O! nothing earthly save the ray
> (Thrown back from flowers) of Beauty's eye,
> As in those gardens where the day
> Springs from the gems of Circassy—
> O! nothing earthly save the thrill
> Of melody in woodland rill—
> Or (music of the passion-hearted)
> Joy's voice so peacefully departed
> That like the murmur in the shell,
> Its echo dwelleth and will dwell—
> Oh, nothing of the dross of ours—
> Yet all the beauty—all the flowers
> That list our Love, and deck our bowers—
> Adorn yon world afar, afar—
> The wandering star.
>
> (Stovall, p. 25)

This poem alternates between poetic passages of great beauty and obscure and rough lines. Bonaparte believes that "Al Aaraaf" was based on Poe's "ancient passion for astronomy": "This passion for astronomy seizes many a child and adolescent when education demands the repression of instinctual urges, for the sky is the bourne of those who seek escape from earthly realities; realities to which, in certain ways, Poe was never to return" (p. 41).

Astronomy is a branch of science that provides youngsters, particularly, with many imaginative possibilities for

flights of fancy. What better place to resolve one's conflicts
than in a great beyond of infinite hopes and dreams? If
one is to carry this idea to a finer point in Freudian theory,
Marie Bonaparte's statement is most significant: "The
passion for astronomy in the young and in adolescents
indicates an attempt, under educative' pressure, to escape
from the tormenting violence of 'guilt' laden sex, and
bathe in the calmness of infinite space" (p. 594) .[21] And
like an astronomer Poe was careful with his work and
precise in his poems. For Poe's claims to poetic genius
rest primarily on a small volume of verse; he was constantly working over and refining his poetry.[22]

As in the work of the astronomer who deals with precision, order, and speculation, there was another dimension
to Poe's work, as previously suggested. He was concerned
with beauty: "He sought, not the varied pleasures of the
world, but the interpretation of Beauty alone, the highest
form of which he felt to be linked always with melancholy"
(Pruette, p. 381) .

One of the themes of Poe's poems is a desire to escape
from the inequities and imperfections of this mortal world
into a land of surcease, hope, joy, and complete childhood
imagination. He speaks to the singing angel, Israfel, in
the poem by the same name, as follows:

> Yes, Heaven is thine; but this
> Is a world of sweets and sours;

---

21. This discussion leads directly into fantasy and the life of the artist.
See Freud's discussion of this point in *A General Introduction to Psycho-
Analysis,* pp. 327–28. For those interested in the psychoanalytic interpretation of the artist, the following will be helpful: Sigmund Freud, *Moses
and Monotheism,* trans. Katherine Jones (New York: Vintage Books, Inc.,
1955) ; and Sigmund Freud, *Leonardo da Vinci: A Psycho-Sexual Study
of an Infantile Reminiscence,* trans. A. A. Brill (New York: Random
House, Inc., 1947) .

22. Stovall in the *Poems* has interesting comments on the text of Poe's
poetry in this regard and is most complete as to variant readings and
textual notes.

> Our flowers are merely—flowers,
> And the shadow of thy perfect bliss
> Is the sunshine of ours.
>
> If I could dwell
> Where Israfel
> Hath dwelt, and he where I,
> He might not sing so wildly well
> A mortal melody,
> While a bolder note than this might swell
> From my lyre within the sky.[23]

(Stovall, p. 49)

The escape into Elysian fields and the entire process of day-dreaming is, according to psychoanalytic theory, closely linked with a desire for a return to an omnipotent state of life where the pleasure principle fully operates and where the individual is in a constant state of wish-fulfillment.[24] "The poet would change places with the angel if only he could, for he feels hampered only by his human condition, not by his genius."[25]

---

23. Harry Levin has also linked "Israfel" with Poe's "The Fall of the House of Usher," "through the quoted metaphor comparing the heart to a lute. Roderick's heartstrings vibrate to the decline, the catalepsy, and the interment of Madeline. Heralded by a reading from a romance, she emerges from the vault in her bloody shroud, and brother and sister share their death-agonies." (pp. 159–60)

24. Joseph Wood Krutch in "The Strange Case of Poe" has captured some of the dynamics associated with this personality phenomenon and connected it with Poe's stories. "First reasoning in order to escape feeling and then seizing upon the idea of reason as an explanation of the mystery of his own character, Poe invented the detective story in order that he might not go mad." (p. 356)

25. Buranelli, p. 98. D. H. Lawrence has also made a keen observation of this phenomenon from the standpoint of man's survival, though he specifically refers to Poe in the following passages: "Poe had a pretty bitter doom. Doomed to seethe down his soul in a great continuous convulsion of disintegration, and doomed to register the process. And then doomed to be abused for it, when he had performed some of the bitterest tasks of human experience, that can be asked of a man. Necessary tasks, too. For the human soul must suffer its own disintegration, *consciously,* if ever it is to survive." *Studies in Classic American Literature* (New York: Thomas Seltzer Inc., 1923), p. 65.

It should be remembered that psychoanalytically oriented criticism lays major emphasis on unconscious determinants to explain underlying factors about human
behavior and activities. Dreams often hide from the individual much of the meaning of his motives and wishes.
Marie Bonaparte explained this in terms of the creative
artist as follows:

> Of all the devices employed by the dreamwork, that
> of the *displacement of psychic intensities*—apart from
> one exception—is the most freely used in the elaboration
> of works of art, doubtless because such displacement is
> generally dictated by the moral censor, which is more
> active in our waking thoughts than in sleep. The con-
> ceiving and writing of literary works are conscious
> activities, and the less the author guesses of the hidden
> themes in his works, the likelier are they to be truly
> creative.[26]

Poe's endeavors to escape from the feeling of being
doomed did not prevent him from writing excellent prose
and beautiful verse. His poetry abounds with images of
beauty and probably forms part of his own wish ideal as
regards the beautiful. But the beautiful is often sur-
rounded with the desolate, death, loneliness, and other
realistic aspects of life. And with it all Poe was an excellent craftsman.[27]

The first stanza of "The City in the Sea" is a fine example of Poe's perceptive powers combined with technical
skill to bring out some poignant lines about death.

---

26. "Poe and the Function of Literature," in *Art and Psychoanalysis*,
ed. William Phillips (Cleveland: The World Publishing Company, 1963) ,
p. 61. Also see Marie Bonaparte, *The Life and Works of Edgar Allan
Poe: A Psycho-Analytic Interpretation*, p. 645.

27. No less an authority than Baudelaire, who was responsible for intro-
ducing Poe to the French, recognized Poe's skill, versatility, and crafts-
manship as a writer. See *Baudelaire on Poe*, trans. and ed. Lois and
Francis E. Hyslop, Jr. (State College, Pa.: Bald Eagle Press, 1952) .

Lo! Death has reared himself a throne
In a strange city lying alone
Far down within the dim West,
Where the good and the bad and the worst and the best
Have gone to their eternal rest.
There shrines and palaces and towers
(Time-eaten towers that tremble not!)
Resemble nothing that is ours.
Around, by lifting winds forgot,
Resignedly beneath the sky
The melancholy waters lie.[28]

(Stovall, p. 50)

Pruette is of the opinion that "City in the Sea" is "a picture of beauty desolated, of death reigning in the courts of life and love" ("A Psycho-Analytical Study of Edgar Allan Poe," p. 383). One thing seems certain about Poe's treatment of death in his poetry. His employment of the imagery of death along with that of sleep and dream-like states has led Roy Harvey Pearce to remark: "Poe is quite obviously the poet of dream-work."[29] Incidentally, death and death-wishes frequently appear in dreams.

In "The Sleeper" a lady is asleep, presumably dead, as we read the following lines:

---

28. All through this poem death reigns supreme in love and life. One can never forget, as Faust did, that he must not tarry for a moment. In "The Interpretation of Dreams" Freud explains that the child's concept of death is alien to that of the adult. To the child, being dead means being gone. The child has generally been spared the sight of much suffering which precedes death. To the child's way of looking at things, according to Freud, the departed one ceases to trouble the survivors. Nevertheless, one of Freud's main underlying themes in one of his works is that the fear of death is closely related to the fear of being forsaken or deserted. The individual feels there will be an end to protection against every danger. Furthermore, the fear of death is closely related to the fear of being castrated. See Sigmund Freud, *The Problem of Anxiety*, trans. H. A. Bunker (New York: The Psychoanalytic Quarterly Press and W. W. Norton & Company, Inc., 1936).

29. *The Continuity of American Poetry* (Princton: Princeton University Press, 1961), p. 141.

The lady sleeps! Oh, may her sleep,
Which is enduring, so be deep!
Heaven have her in its sacred keep!
This chamber changed for one more holy,
This bed for one more melancholy,
I pray to God that she may lie
Forever with unopened eye,
While the pale sheeted ghosts go by!

(Stovall, p. 53)

In referring to "The Sleeper" Pruette is of the opinion
that Poe "is occupied with his dominant theme, the link-
ing of sex and death" (p. 385). The theme of love and
death comes out again and again in such poems as "To
One in Paradise," the "Sonnet to Zante," "Leonore,"
"Ulalume," "Annabel Lee," and the universal favorite,
"The Raven." There are many psychoanalytic, especially
Freudian, overtones in all of these poems as indeed there
are in most of Poe's works.

Probably no psychoanalytically oriented critic could
offer a more telling explanation of death and beauty than
does Poe himself. In his exposition of the composition and
conception of "The Raven," Poe writes:

I had now gone so far as the conception of a Raven,
the bird of ill-omen, monotonously repeating the one
word "Nevermore" at the conclusion of each stanza in a
poem of melancholy tone, and in length about one hundred lines. Now, never losing sight of the object—
supremeness or perfection at all points, I asked myself—
"Of all melancholy topics what, according to the *universal* understanding of mankind, is the most melancholy?" Death, was the obvious reply. "And when," I
said, "is this most melancholy of topics most poetical?"
From what I have already explained at some length the
answer here also is obvious—"When it most closely allies
itself to *Beauty:* the death then of a beautiful woman is

unquestionably the most poetical topic in the world, and equally is it beyond doubt that the lips best suited for such topic are those of a bereaved lover."[30]

Naturally, such an explanation is bound to arouse all kinds of Freudian psychoanalytic speculations. One of the experiences that would naturally be sought out in this regard would be Poe's early years. Poe's early life with women and even his later relations with women were filled with a good deal of tragedy and unhappiness of all kinds. Beauty to Poe was evidently tied to something in his psyche, which was to be lost, was not to be enjoyed, and above all was to bring a good deal of suffering. Beauty really meant dead beauty, as is clearly shown in his poems.

Poe's parents died early and under very unpleasant circumstances. His mother was reputed to be most gifted and beautiful. At a most impressionable age came another blow—the death of Mrs. Helen Stanard—his first Helen. Later, came the death of his foster mother, followed by the loss of three sweethearts, and the six years of fear for the life of his wife Virginia, who finally died at the age of twenty-five in 1847.[31] Beautiful women to Poe were meant to be written about but never to feel secure with. "Little wonder, then, that he wrote of the death of beautiful women" (Pruette, p. 386).

---

30. "The Philosophy of Composition," in Quinn and O'Neill, eds., 2:982.

31. All of these items are treated in the various biographies already mentioned. Three of the biographies tend to be more psychological than the others—those by Bonaparte, Krutch, and Robertson.

3
Walt Whitman

SOME PSYCHODYNAMIC CONSIDERATIONS OF WHITMAN

The content of his immense literary output reveals Walt Whitman's innermost feeling with unusual candor. In addition to his production, there is something about Whitman's life that seems to arouse interest in the creative artist, particularly the artist as a poet.[1] Henry Seidel Canby has dealt with this phenomenon by pointing out the following:

> For the truth of the matter is that a satisfactory biography of Whitman must be essentially a biography of an inner life and of the mysterious creative processes of poetry. It was in Whitman's inner life that the great things, some of them heroic, happened. It is his inner life that infused into the 'Leaves of Grass' such greatness as it possesses, which is far more than his contemporaries guessed. When the middle-aged poet wrote of the 'Leaves,' 'Who touches this touches a man,' he was tell-

1. The impact of Whitman's production can be gauged from the critical writings and reviews his work has engendered. See Evie Allison Allen, "A Check List of Whitman Publications 1945–1960," in Gay Wilson Allen, *Walt Whitman as Man, Poet, and Legend* (Carbondale: Southern Illinois University Press, 1961), pp. 179–244. Also, a review of Whitman research and criticism can be found in Willard Thorp, "Walt Whitman," in *Eight American Authors: A Review of Research and Criticism*, ed. Floyd Stovall (New York: W. W. Norton & Company, Inc., 1963), pp. 271–318. Each year the material on Whitman enlarges, as is attested by various annual biographies.

ing the literal truth. We all distrust interpretive biographies, but the biography of Whitman has to be interpretive, because the sources for an account of what is really significant in his life are in his writings. Walt's visible life in the theatres of New York, on the streets of Brooklyn, in the hospitals of Washington, and in his room at Camden is a by-product of that inner life, which itself was conditioned by influences as much spiritual as physical. And the American that he created in his poems, out of what his eyes saw and his ears heard, was meant from the beginning to be a symbol of a faith and a dream.[2]

Whitman lived from May 31, 1819 to March 26, 1892, a ripe age of more than seven decades. Enduring the pains of a growing country, the Civil War, and a rising industrial society, Whitman's faith and dream was essentially childlike in its hope for fulfillment. It is the kind of stuff from which great ideas and great literature seem to spring.

Richard Chase, who differs somewhat in his point of view from Canby, expresses his thoughts about Whitman as follows:

---

2. *Walt Whitman an American* (Boston: Houghton Mifflin Co., 1943), p. 2. Canby's statement is very close to the heart of Freud's paper, "The Relation of the Poet to Day-Dreaming," in which poetic production is traced to children's play and day-dreaming. Freud writes: "Now the writer does the same as the child at play; he creates a world of phantasy which he takes very seriously; that is, he invests it with a great deal of affect, while separating it sharply from reality. Language has preserved this relationship between children's play and poetic creation. It designates certain kinds of imaginative creation, concerned with tangible objects and capable of representation, as 'plays'; the people who present them are called 'players.' The unreality of this poetical world of imagination, however, has very important consequences for literary technique; for many things which if they happened in real life could produce no pleasure can nevertheless give enjoyment in a play—many emotions which are essentially painful may become a source of enjoyment to the spectators and hearers of a poet's work." *Collected Papers*, ed. Ernest Jones (London: The Hogarth Press and the Institute of Psycho-Analysis, 1949), 4:174. Of interest here, too, is the following study: Edwin Haviland Miller, *Walt Whitman's Poetry: A Psychological Journey* (Boston: Houghton Mifflin Company, 1968).

Whitman is hard to pin down. He resists identities,
especially those which disguise the fact that his personality was so considerably indeterminate, neurotic, power
conscious, furtive, given alternately to dreams of order
and of annihilation and that despite all his absurdities
he was a great poet and, in ways open to definition, a
profound and salutary revolutionary force in our culture. To remember that Whitman resists identities
must be the minimum responsibility of anyone who
presumes to write about him.[3]

It is not the aim here to "psychoanalyze" Whitman. It
should be noted however that he not only antedated
Freud in time but also appears to have done so in his clear
conceptions of many of Freud's insights. What is more,
there is something so special about personalities like Whitman that one must guard against the temptation to draw
erroneous inferences. Hence,

We often think of a man's physical life as his *real*
existence, and regard his subjective life as shadowy,
illusive, unsubstantial. And so it may be. But Walt
Whitman's aesthetic and spiritual life was so real to him
that he often himself confused the physical and the
psychological realms of his experience—or at least wrote
and spoke of them in such a way as to cause his readers
and biographers to confuse them. One of his greatest
literary ambitions was to make his poems seem so real
that the reader would forget he was reading a book.[4]

The above quotation finds expression in the poem "So
Long," as follows:

> Camerado, this is no book,
> Who touches this touches a man,
> (Is it night? are we here together alone?)

3. *Walt Whitman Reconsidered* (New York: William Sloane Associates,
Inc., 1955) , p. 17.
4. Allen, *Walt Whitman as Man, Poet, and Legend*, p. 3.

It is I you hold and who holds you,
I spring from the pages into your arms—
decease calls me forth.[5]

Here we have the blending of the physical and the subjective, the coming together of body and spirit, which has
provided much discussion and thought about Whitman's
kinship to eastern philosophy.[6] As previously suggested,
Whitman's being the complicated individual he was
helped to create much of the mystery and speculation sur-
rounding his biography. Allen points this up as follows:

> Later biographers and critics of Whitman, however,
> were to discover that the poet himself had made it
> difficult to understand the author of *Leaves of Grass*.
> Jean Catel, the late French biographer, argued that
> Whitman deliberately created myths about himself, a
> view elaborated a few years later by the Danish critic,
> Frederick Schyberg. Henry Seidel Canby, one of our
> best American biographers, found two Whitmans, the
> person known to his family and friends and the symbol-
> ical self of his poems. Malcolm Cowley went a step
> further and wrote of three Whitmans. I would say that
> if one searched thoroughly for the man behind the first
> pronoun in "Song of Myself" and other major lyrics in
> *Leaves of Grass,* he could find as many as five or six
> personalities; for although the lyric is the most personal
> form of poetic art, it is also a kind of dream, and the "I"
> can assume many roles—as it does even in *Leaves of
> Grass.* (p. 4)

In line with the above remarks, it must be emphasized
that one should guard against the temptation of alluding

---

5. Walt Whitman, *Leaves of Grass,* ed. Emory Holloway (Garden City,
N.Y.: Doubleday & Company, Inc., 1926) , p. 418. Unless otherwise indicated, the Whitman poems quoted are from this Inclusive Edition.

6. For an interesting and brief discussion on this point, see Arthur E.
Briggs, *Walt Whitman: Thinker and Artist* (New York: Philosophical
Library, 1952) , pp. 85–110.

to Whitman in psychiatric terms. Whitman was a man beset like most men with problems of his own. We are primarily interested in him because he left us a rich literary heritage, not because of any possible personality aberration.

In 1921, Emory Holloway published the *Uncollected Poetry and Prose of Walt Whitman*. This work contained the poet's early journalistic writings, Whitman's private notebooks, and juvenilia in poetry and prose. Holloway and his co-workers continued to examine material credited to Whitman; this examination also included material hypothetically accredited to Whitman. When Holloway was ready to publish the biography of the poet, *Whitman, An Interpretation in Narrative* (1926), he was probably more aware of the poet's writings than any other contemporary. His was the first complete account of Walt Whitman's experience as a journalist and editor. With a psychological bent reminiscent of orthodox psychoanalytic understanding, "and on the natural assumption that the child is father to the man, he attempted to explain the mature poet in terms of his early life and intellectual development."[7]

Making many suggestive interpretations concerning the poet's psychological makeup, Holloway's biography gave impetus to others speculating on Whitman's psyche. Jean Catel in *Walt Whitman: La Naissance du Poète* delved into the depths of the poet's soul for a psychoanalytical autopsy. Interestingly enough, what follows is practically a page from a psychoanalyst's case-book:

> The myself that Whitman 'celebrates' on each page . . . is the projection of the unconscious. If in reading Whitman's work, the reader will replace mentally the *I* or

---

7. Gay Wilson Allen, *Walt Whitman Handbook* (Chicago: Packard and Company, 1946), p. 55. This book contains a most interesting discussion in Chapter I, "The Growth of Walt Whitman Biography," pp. 1–103.

the *myself* by 'my unconscious' while giving to this word the dynamic sense which we have indicated, then he will understand better: first, the origin, the profound reason for the first edition of *Leaves of Grass;* second, the end, what certain critics have called the messianic in Whitman.[8]

And Gay Wilson Allen observes of Whitman: "Being in his conscious mind agitated by a sense of failure, frustration, and loneliness, his poetic imagination returns to an idealized childhood of peace, innocence, and purity, and it is then that he feels in his soul that he is the equal of God" *(Walt Whitman Handbook,* p. 62) .

PSYCHOANALYTICALLY ORIENTED CRITICISM OF
SELECTED WHITMAN POETRY

Critic Gustav Bychowski feels that since Whitman reveals his most intimate feelings and ideas in his poetry and prose, "he offers, therefore, a unique opportunity for the study of artistic expression and sublimation and he is a great temptation to an analyst fascinated by the problem of artistic creation."[9] Bychowski proceeds to concern himself with an understanding of Whitman via his poetry. Particularly, he is interested in "the power of the creative

---

8. Text translated here from the French by Allen in his *Walt Whitman Handbook,* p. 62.

9. "Walt Whitman: A Study in Sublimation," in *Psychoanalysis and the Social Sciences,* ed. Géza Róheim (New York: International Universities Press, Inc., 1951) , 3: 223. The term "sublimation" as employed by Bychowski in the above passage and in his title refers to the following: "The process through which the excessive excitations from individual sexual sources are discharged and utilized in other spheres, so that no small enhancement of mental capacity results from a predisposition which is dangerous as such." See Nandor Fodor and Frank Gaynor, eds., *Freud: Dictionary of Psychoanalysis* (New York: The Philosophical Library, Inc., 1950) , p. 178. Also, *The Basic Writings of Sigmund Freud,* ed. A. A. Brill (New York: Random House, Inc., 1938) , pp. 18–19, 584, 603, 625–26.

ego to deal with its difficulties, to make use of the most disturbing elemental forces" (p. 223) . And in addition to the concept of *sublimation,* Bychowski employs two other psychoanalytic mechanisms in his psychoanalytically oriented observations of Whitman's poetry. These are the mechanisms of *introjection*[10] and *identification.*[11] How vividly Whitman expressed these mechanisms in his poetry, according to Bychowski, can be seen from the following lines of his poem, entitled, "There Was a Child Went Forth":

There was a child went forth every day,
And the first object he look'd upon, that object he became,
And that object became part of him for the day or a certain
    part of the day,
Or for many years or stretching cycles of years.
                          (Leaves of Grass, p. 306)

    "This process then applies more specifically to his parents" (Bychowski, p. 223) . He goes on to quote the following lines:

His own parents, he that had father'd him and she that had
    conceiv'd him in her womb and birth'd him,
They gave this child more of themselves than that,

---

10. The term introjection was coined by the Hungarian psychoanalyst S. Ferenczi and Freud gives him credit for this. See Sigmund Freud, *Collected Papers,* ed. Ernest Jones (London: The Hogarth Press and The Institute of Psycho-Analysis, 1949) , IV, 78. It means "absorption of the environment into the ego so that external events are reacted to as if they were internal and part of one's personality." J. S. Van Teslaar, ed. *An Outline of Psychoanalysis* (New York: The Modern Library, Inc., 1925) , p. 381.

11. "First, identification is the original form of emotional tie with an object; secondly, in a regressive way it becomes a substitute for a libidinal object tie, as it were by means of the introjection of the object into the ego; and thirdly, it may arise with every new perception of a common quality shared with some other person who is not an object of the sexual instinct." See Fodor and Gaynor, p. 93. Also, Sigmund Freud, *Group Psychology and the Analysis of the Ego,* trans. James Strachey (London: The Hogarth Press and the Institute of Psycho-Analysis, 1948) , p. 65.

They gave him afterward every day, they became part of
him.[12]

(Leaves of Grass, pp. 306–07)

To summarize briefly Bychowski's observations thus far,
one can infer that (1) Whitman understood human development to be a continuous process from childhood to
adulthood, (2) the environment played an important part
in the child's development, (3) the role of the parents
was particularly important in the development of one's
personality, and (4) the phenomenon of identification
was the underlying substance of the child's development.

Though the above easily suggests that Whitman clearly
understood phases of human growth and development,
Bychowski raises the question about Whitman's "acute
feelings of depersonalization." He continues to use "There
Was a Child Went Forth" as his point of discussion and
writes about the following passage:

The family usages, the language, the company, the furni-
ture, the yearning and swelling heart,
Affection that will not be gainsay'd, the sense of what is
real, the thought if after all it should prove unreal,
The doubts of day-time and the doubts of night-time, the
curious whether and how,
Whether that which appears so is so, or is it all flashes and
specks?
Men and women crowding fast in the streets, if they are
not flashes and specks what are they?

(Leaves of Grass, p. 307)

The above lines, according to Bychowski, are part and

---

12. In this context, another definition and explanation of the term
identification is pertinent: ". . . that one ego becomes like another, one
which results in the first ego behaving itself in certain respects in the same
way as the second; it imitates it, and as it were takes it into itself. This
identification has been not inappropriately compared with the oral can-
nabalistic incorporation of another person." See Sigmund Freud, *New
Introductory Lectures on Psycho-Analysis*, trans. W. J. Sprott (New
York: W. W. Norton & Company, Inc., 1933), p. 90.

parcel of an overriding frustration on the part of Whitman. "Since the same essential doubt of reality recurs time and again in his poems with a poignant awareness of its actuality, it appears that it has never been overcome completely and continues to threaten the ego" ("Walt Whitman: A Study in Sublimation," p. 224). Evidently, this doubting emerges into a wondering attitude about one's identity beyond the grave. For in his poem "Of the Terrible Doubt of Appearances," Whitman exclaims in anguish:

Of the terrible doubt of appearances,
Of the uncertainty after all, that we may be deluded,
That may-be reliance and hope are but speculations after
    all,
That may-be identity beyond the grave is a beautiful
    fable only,
May-be the things I perceive, the animals, plants, men,
    hills, shining and flowing waters,
The skies of day and night, colors, densities, forms, may-be
    these are (as doubtless they are) only apparitions, and
    the real something has yet to be known.
(How often they dart out of themselves as if to confound
    me and mock me![13]
                              (*Leaves of Grass*, pp. 100–101)

13. At the time of the publication of these lines, Whitman was a mature, middle-aged individual of forty-eight. One can argue that death, along with immortality, becomes a "normal" subject of thought in the middle years. Nevertheless, one should not get the feeling that Whitman here is an arch pessimist. A person of Whitman's outlook may possess doubt as a healthy and creative aspect of personality. For in spite of many personal difficulties, Whitman's underlying attitude was a broad optimistic one; it was a positive and optimistic affirmation of life. "A glowing love for humanity, which has its root in the physical no less surely than it transcends the physical, is the central emotion of Whitman's being, the inspiration of all he wrote." See Ernest de Selincourt, *Wordsworthian and Other Studies* (New York: Russell & Russell, Inc., 1964), p. 141. It is also interesting to remember that one of the greatest psychologists saw fit to set forth Whitman as an example of one whose life had a breadth and vision on a "large objective scale." See William James, *Talks to Teachers on Psychology: and to Students on Some of Life's Ideals* (New York: W. W. Norton & Company, Inc., 1958), pp. 160–63.

"Of the Terrible Doubt of Appearances" is part of the Whitman series of poems known as the Calamus poems. Paul Lauter believes this group of poems contains many characteristics of traditional sonnet sequences. In spite of all other claims, "the Poet wishes to be remembered only as a lover and a celebrator of love, discounting other kinds of fame as superficial."[14]

This view is somewhat elaborated upon by Frederik Schyberg, who believes that while Whitman is expressing doubt about his identity after death, he finds comfort and support in "my lovers, my dear friends,"[15] in the following line:

To me these and the like of these are curiously answer'd
     by my lovers, my dear friends,
                              (*Leaves of Grass,* p. 101)

Evidently then, Whitman comes to terms with the fear of being deluded about his identity after death by resolving "such doubts in the consciousness"[16] in the way revealed in the lines immediately above and in the following concluding lines from "Of the Terrible Doubt of Appearances":

I cannot answer the question of appearances or that of
     identity beyond the grave,
But I walk or sit indifferent, I am satisfied,
He ahold of my hand has completely satisfied me.
                              (*Leaves of Grass,* p. 101)

James E. Miller, Jr. believes that "Of the Terrible Doubt of Appearances" is Whitman's way of indicating "that, in

14. "Walt Whitman: Lover and Comrade," *American Imago* 16 (Winter 1959) : 428–29.

15. *Walt Whitman,* trans. Evie Allison Allen (New York: Columbia University Press, 1951) , p. 177.

16. This is the view held by Briggs, p. 466.

the doubt and uncertainty about reality and 'identity be-yond the grave,' such love grants 'untold and untellable wisdom,' a knowledge similar to the intuitive knowledge of the mystic."[17]

Psychoanalytically oriented critics have also spent a good deal of time conjecturing on Whitman's poem, "Out of the Cradle Endlessly Rocking." The following stanza of the poem contains many of the items which make for psy-choanalytic observations:

Out of the cradle endlessly rocking,
Out of the mocking-bird's throat, the musical shuttle,
Out of the Ninth-month midnight,
Over the sterile sands and the fields beyond, where the
    child leaving his bed wander'd alone, bareheaded,
    barefoot,
Down from the shower'd halo,
Up from the mystic play of shadows twining and twisting
    as if they were alive,
Out from the patches of briers and blackberries,
From the memories of the bird that chanted to me,
From your memories sad brother, from the fitful risings
    and fallings I heard,
From under that yellow half-moon late-risen and swollen
    as if with tears,
From those beginning notes of yearning and love there in
    the mist,
From the thousand responses of my heart never to cease,
From the myriad thence-arous'd words,
From the word stronger and more delicious than any,
From such as now they start the scene revisiting,
As a flock, twittering, rising, or overhead passing,
Borne hither, ere all eludes me, hurriedly,
A man, yet by these tears a little boy again,
Throwing myself on the sand, confronting the waves,
I, chanter of pains and joys, uniter of here and hereafter,

---

17. *A Critical Guide to Leaves of Grass* (Chicago: University of Chi-cago Press, 1957), p. 65.

Taking all hints to use them, but swiftly leaping beyond
   them,
A reminiscence sing.

(Leaves of Grass, p. 210)

Bychowski views the above as follows:

This poem taps the deep unconscious sources so as to
convey to the reader the world of early emotions, well-
nigh the beginnings of individual self-awareness, the
birth of the ego, born in pain of love. ("Walt Whitman:
A Study in Sublimation," pp. 225–226)

According to this critic, the above lines of "Out of the
Cradle Endlessly Rocking" indicate that an unhappy male
bird is wailing the loss of his mate, during which time a
song is unleashed in the beginning bard, Walt. The future
poet then seems later in the poem to identify himself
with the unfortunate lover as well as with his lost com-
panion.

Another view of this poem from a psychoanalytically
oriented vantage point is that of Neil D. Isaacs. He writes:

"Out of the Cradle Endlessly Rocking" is a veritable
Whitman's sampler of his typical themes and devices.
The poet sings a reminiscence of a boyhood experience,
a summer's observations of a bird who lost his mate and
sang of his loss in songs which the poet now translates.
But the reason the experience is important is for what it
meant to the boy, not the bird.[18]

Isaacs believes that "bird and boy-translator, pour forth
their anguished, passionate, vainly sensual love-call" (p.
105). He goes on to say:

   Gerunds (risings and fallings, yearning), present

---

18. "The Autoerotic Metaphor in Joyce, Sterne, Lawrence, Stevens
and Whitman," *Literature and Psychology* 15 (Spring 1965) : 105.

participles prepositions (up, out, over, from, from under) are the principal parts of speech bearing the meta-
phorical train of thought. But I'll confine my list to some
of the more suggestive idioms and bits of phrasing. For
example, as the bird imagines his mate in shapes in the
foam and the moon, the boy imagines "white arms out
in the breakers" and the moon to be "heavy with love."
(p. 105)

Furthermore, the autoerotic manifestations of this poem
are also seen, according to Isaacs, both in the "rocking
motion" of the title "Out of the Cradle Endlessly Rocking"
and in the "furiously charging rhythms." Of course, all of
this leads eventually to one extended musical metaphor.

In commenting about the beauty of this poem from a
psychoanalytically oriented standpoint, Bychowski observes:

When we reduce the poignant beauty of this poem to
its unconscious core, we see the first separation of infancy, the first anguish of infantile love underlying all
the future pain of love. Sweet death emerges then as
the great benefactor, as a supreme salvation, since it
promises a reunion with the beloved mother, earth,
sea, and maybe the universe. ("Walt Whitman: A Study
in Sublimation," p. 226)

The concept of death in "Out of the Cradle Endlessly
Rocking," "Of the Terrible Doubt of Appearances," and
many other poems, has led D. H. Lawrence to make the
following observations:

Whitman would not have been the great poet he is if
he had not taken the last steps and looked over into
death. Death, the last merging, that was the goal of his
manhood.[19]

---

19. *Studies in Classic American Literature* (New York: Thomas Seltzer
Inc., 1923), p. 170.

Whitman's concern with death appears to have as its base a concern with immortality. In this regard, it is also important to note that reassurance is one way of bolstering one's ego. Whitman does not seem to tire of pouring out reassurances for his own as well as for the reader's benefit. Again, there seems to be connected with this phenomenon an intense feeling for immortality. In the final verse of "To Think of Time," Whitman writes:

I swear I think now that every thing without exception
    has an eternal soul!
The trees have, rooted in the ground! the weeds of the sea
    have! the animals!

I swear I think there is nothing but immortality!
That the exquisite scheme is for it, and the nebulous float
    is for it, and the cohering is for it!
And all preparation is for it—and identity is for it—and life
    and materials are altogether for it![20]

(*Leaves of Grass,* p. 368)

In commenting about the poem "To Think of Time," Bychowski observes the following about Whitman:

> Reassurances which he does not tire of pouring out
> for his own benefit, even more than for the benefit of
> his reader, indicate an intense fear of personal annihila-
> tion. He who sang some of the most poignantly beauti-
> ful hymns in praise of Death, seems to fear it as intensely

---

20. Since immortality is tied directly to concepts of life and death, Whitman's lines carry within them a sense of reassurance, reminiscent of Freud's words in his work, "Interpretation of Dreams." He comments on death as follows: " 'To depart' is one of the most frequent and one of the most readily established of the death-symbols. The dream there- fore says consolingly: 'Reassure yourself, you are not going to die (to depart) ,' just as the examination-dream calms us by saying: 'Don't be afraid; this time, too, nothing will happen to you.' The difficulty in understanding both kinds of dreams is due to the fact that the anxiety is attached precisely to the expression of consolation." See *The Basic Writings,* p. 387.

as a threat to his much-beloved ego. He is frightened by
the passage of time which conveys to things and people
the character of transition. ("Walt Whitman: A Study
in Sublimation," p. 225)

Bychowski also goes on to make the point that Whitman's fear of death was, in psychoanalytic terms, "a reac-
tion of his ego" to his early yearning for supreme salvation
via love through death. "It was the fright of annihilation
for which it was secretly longing, as a way of restoring
the lost dual unity with his mother" (pp. 227–28).

However, Whitman's hymn of self-affirmation, called
"Song of Myself," exalts the body and the psychological
ego and makes readers believe in the ultimate end of
life—affirmation. The poem also celebrates the joy over
oneself, as noted in these opening lines:

I celebrate myself, and sing myself,
And what I assume you shall assume,
For every atom belonging to me as good belongs to you.
(Leaves of Grass, p. 24)

And later in the poem we read:

The real or fancied indifference of some man or woman
  I love,
The sickness of one of my folks or of myself, or ill-doing
  or loss or lack of money, or depressions or
  exaltations,
Battles, the horrors of fratricidal war, the fever of
  doubtful news, the fitful events;
These come to me days and nights and go from me again,
But they are not the Me myself.
(Leaves of Grass, p. 27)

Bychowski believes that there is a high degree of nar-

cissism[21] revealed by Whitman in this poem. A. A. Brill
sharpens his psychoanalytically oriented comments by con-
necting this poem with other Whitman poems and writes:

> Walt Whitman's narcissism expressed in the 'Song
> About Myself,' and his homosexuality expressed in his
> 'Calamus Poems,' emanating as they do from the poet's
> infantile components, are not only comprehensible, but
> even touching, whereas "Tender Buttons" or "Pink
> Melon Joy" leaves us cold or can inspire us only with
> laughter.[22]

In a discussion of Whitman and some of his poetry,
another psychoanalytically oriented critic, Paul Lauter,
offers the following footnote comment, which is in contra-
distinction to the definite view suggested by Brill in the
previous quotation:

> I do not suggest that Whitman had any overt homosex-
> ual experiences; there is no evidence whatever to
> indicate that he was, in our sense of the word, a
> "homosexual." I do assert, however, that he sought
> from men the kind of day to day warmth and intimacy
> usually found by a man in relations with a woman. The
> debate about Whitman's sexual nature has been con-
> siderably muddled by failure to distinguish between
> urge and practice and by the application of twentieth-
> century psychological abstractions to nineteenth-century
> realities. ("Walt Whitman: Lover and Comrade,"
> p. 433)

---

21. Closely involved with the Freudian concept of identification is that
of "narcissism." For our present discussion we can think of this term
as related to erotic feelings aroused by one's own body or personality
leading to a high degree of self-love. Often this is blended with a high
degree of egoism. This topic is discussed in the following: Sigmund
Freud, *A General Introduction to Psycho-Analysis*, trans. Joan Riviere
(Garden City, N.Y.: Garden City Publishing Company, Inc., 1943), pp.
361–62.

22. "Poetry as an Oral Outlet," *The Psychoanalytic Review* 18 (October 1931) : 378.

Whitman's poetry is filled with allusions to bodily processes, sex, love, the ego, and a host of psychoanalytically charged words. As indicated elsewhere, the temptation to draw conclusions psychoanalytically is fraught with many pitfalls. In light of this, the last sentence of the above quotation from Lauter on the need for circumspection along psychoanalytic lines becomes of historical interest also.

As Richard Chase, another psychoanalytically oriented critic, has pointed out, an understanding of Whitman, regardless from what vantage point one may be studying him, demands a clear awareness that "Whitman is the representative of his country because he and his poetry mirror in a radical if incomplete way the very contradictions of American civilization."[23] His beliefs, his ambiguities, his wit, his sorrows, optimism, joys, and faith in man and in democracy force one "to understand him in his contradictions" (p. 46). Modern depth psychology, particularly psychoanalysis, makes a serious attempt at reconciling, through understanding, the contradictions in human behavior.

In reconciling personality differences inherent in one's own being, the psychoanalyst especially concerns himself with infantile repressions and guilt feelings, in order to clarify one's emotional situation. Bychowski, speaking like the psychoanalyst he is, views "Song of Myself" in the following light:

> Exaltation over the bodily ego seems a clear manifestation not only of its rediscovery but of salvation from infantile repressions and feelings of guilt. It is important to pay close attention to all those processes since they have paved the way for the powerful thrust of sublima-

23. *Walt Whitman* (Minneapolis: University of Minnesota Press, 1961), p. 46.

tion. Here again it is through the study of poetic exalta-
tion as a compensatory mechanism that we can arrive at
the appreciation of the pitfalls of guilt and repression.
From these the poet had to save himself in order not
only to fulfill his mission but even to survive and to
emerge from the depths of dejection.[24] ("Walt Whitman: A Study in Sublimation," p. 230)

In his inaugural address as the first holder of the Chair
of American Literature at Leeds University in England,
Douglas Grant devoted his entire talk to Walt Whitman.
He took note of some of the poet's personality problems
as revealed in his poetry, but made it a point to give wider
interpretation than a limited psychological one. In discussing Whitman's poetry, Grant made the following remark:

> It was easy to write down his attitude as narcissistic,
> but the attentive reader would recognize at once that
> he was being invited to identify himself with the poet;
> that the experiences described were described not to be
> marvelled at but to be shared.[25]

If one follows the above quest for identity with Whitman to its logical conclusion, Bychowski's following comments on "Song of Myself" and "I Sing the Body Electric"
apply equally to the reader: "Liberation from sexual guilt

24. Again, while it is comparatively simple to "analyze" a person's behavior pattern from work that is psychoanalytically tinged, it is important to note that there are different ways of observing a work of poetry.
For example, one critic makes it a point to remind readers that Whitman
enjoyed naming things with childhood glee and with deep, primitive,
poetic feelings. See F. O. Matthiessen, *American Renaissance* (New York:
Oxford University Press, 1941), pp. 517–32. Of interest here too is
Whitman's "Preface to 1855 Edition of 'Leaves of Grass,'" *Leaves of
Grass*, pp. 488–507.

25. *Walt Whitman and His English Admirers.* Lecture Delivered in
the University of Leeds, November 6, 1961 (Leeds: Leeds University
Press, 1962), p. 8. Many American critics have noted this too: Matthiessen,
Pearce, Allen, Feinberg, and others.

and dejection is achieved partly through a sort of cosmic generalization of sex; partly, however, through simple affirmation of things previously feared and despised" ("Walt Whitman: A Study in Sublimation," p. 232).

Although D. H. Lawrence is generally at odds with Whitman's philosophy, one possible feeling on the part of the reader of identification with Whitman's expressed poetic thoughts was observed by Lawrence as follows:

And my soul takes the open road. She meets the souls that are passing, she goes along with the souls that are going her way. And for one and all, she has sympathy. The sympathy of love, the sympathy of hate, the sympathy of simple proximity; all the subtle sympathizings of the incalculable soul, from the bitterest hate to passionate love.[26] (*Studies in Classic American Literature*, pp. 176–77)

How well the above remarks are bound to strike home with the average reader can be seen in the manner in which Whitman includes male and female in the following lines from his poem, "Starting from Paumanok":[27]

I will make the true poem of riches,
To earn for the body and the mind whatever adheres
 and goes forward and is not dropt by death;
I will effuse egotism and show it underlying all, and I
 will be the bard of personality,
And I will show of male and female that either is but the
 equal of the other,
And sexual organs and acts! do you concentrate in me,

26. Lawrence's comments are reminiscent of what James E. Miller, Jr. remarked regarding Whitman's "Song of the Open Road": "The poet's appeal to the reader is an appeal to involvement in all the diversity and hardships of the individualized life." *Walt Whitman* (New York: Twayne Publishers, Inc., 1962), p. 103.
27. An interesting explanation of this poem in terms of its setting in Brooklyn can be found in Frances Winwar, *American Giant: Walt Whitman and His Times* (New York: Harper & Brothers, 1941), pp. 8–18.

for I am determin'd to tell you with courageous clear
     voice to prove you illustrious,
And I will show that there is no imperfection in the pres-
     ent, and can be none in the future,
And I will show that whatever happens to anybody it may
     be turn'd to beautiful results,
And I will show that nothing can happen more beautiful
     than death,
And I will thread a thread through my poems that time
     and events are compact,
And that all the things of the universe are perfect miracles,
     each as profound as any.
                           (*Leaves of Grass,* pp. 18–19)

Whitman appears to have included humanity in his
thinking when he wrote the above lines. "He knew joy
and gladness and the exultation of a healthy body, but he
learned also that all was not happiness in life, that parting
and sorrow, too, formed the heart of experience" (Winwar,
p. 16).

From a psychoanalytically oriented standpoint, Whitman's insights developed from an infantile fixation on
one's self to a higher state of mature development, as observed through his poetry. Bychowski, after much discussion of Whitman's poetry, states:

Thus at last Whitman completely overcame his narcis-
sistic isolation. Blending himself with the splendidly
growing young American democracy, he found a screen
of tremendous magnitude on which to project his own
dearest desires and ideas. In this reunion, he could at
last achieve happiness. He could find and reassert his
own ego, but also his origins from the oceanic and
maternal cradle, the original unity with his mother. He
could love others with all the implications of his love
hungry heart and he could love them without ever stopping to love himself. He could effuse "egotism" and yet

proclaim the religion of brotherhood and true humanity. ("Walt Whitman: A Study in Sublimation," p. 261)

In concluding this discussion it should be stressed that by identifying with all other human beings, Whitman is proclaiming the right of the individual to unfold his personality in accordance with his highest potential. This is what the American psychologist Abraham Maslow refers to as "self-actualization." From this vantage point it is a short step for Whitman to emphasize individuality as the greatest principle of democracy. Furthermore, if one follows psychoanalytic reasoning, as pointed out above in the case of Whitman, certain deductions can be made as to the poet's narcissism. Enmeshing himself within the young and growing democracy, Whitman found a background and foreground upon which to project his innermost desires and ideas. He could expand his ego from a maternal cradle on through loving others without stopping to love himself. Through such identification, he could radiate "egotism" and yet proclaim the brotherhood of humanity.

4

Conrad Aiken

AIKEN'S RELATIONSHIP TO DEPTH PSYCHOLOGY

Of the three poets under discussion, only Conrad Aiken (1889–   ) can be considered a contemporary of Sigmund Freud (1856–1939). Edgar Allan Poe (1809–1849) died seven years before the birth of Freud, and Walt Whitman (1819–1892) died while Freud was still in his thirties, prior to the time when Freud had published his major works. Hence, of the three poets, only Aiken's literary output was realized during a period of world history when depth psychology, particularly psychoanalysis, had a profound influence on an understanding of human behavior.

Furthermore, Aiken's conscious interest in psychoanalysis has often revealed itself in his criticism and literary work, especially in his poetry, where he frequently employed psychological information as part of his theme. This has resulted in critics' centering on Aiken not only as critic and poet, but "psychologist" as well. Louis Untermeyer writes:

> Readers hot for certainties are bound to be bothered by ambivalences and ambiguities. It has been objected that Aiken is too much the analyst for his own—and the reader's—good; that, prompted by the pronouncements

of Freud, he has been unable to resist a central pre-
occupation: the insistence that men live from dream to
dream, from one dubious and always disillusioned ideal
to another.[1]

Of special concern here are the following critics: Beach,
Blackmur, Blanshard, Dillon, Hoffman, Kazin, Moore,
Murray, Pearce, Peterson, Rein, Wells, Whicher, and of
course Freud. To be sure, not all of these individuals are
die-hard critics employing psychoanalytically grounded
tools. They are, however, by virtue of pertinent remarks
about Aiken and/or his work included here as psychoanalytically oriented critics, since their observations fall
within such a purview. However, fully to appreciate the
insights of the critics into the poetry of Aiken, it is necessary to bring out pertinent material about Aiken's background.

Interestingly enough, Aiken's own life seems to be such
that it readily lends itself to psychoanalytic interpretation.
But biographical material on Aiken is presented here for
the sole purpose of examining the poet's relationship to
depth psychology.

Conrad Aiken's life includes a New England heritage,
a Southern background, and an English period of resi-
dency. Born in Savannah, Georgia, August 5, 1889, he was
the first of three sons born to a New England-bred couple,
William and Anna Aiken. "His surname points to the
Scotch blood he shares with his thematic and stylistic an-
cestor Poe."[2]

---

1. "Conrad Aiken: Our Best Known Unread Poet," *Saturday Review*
(November 25, 1967), p. 28. It is to Untermeyer's credit that in this article he does not pinpoint psychology or any one "plausible reason" for
Aiken's inability to attract a large following; rather, he offers a considered
balance of many factors, not the least of which is Aiken's refusal to
popularize himself.
2. Reuel Denney, *Conrad Aiken*, University of Minnesota Pamphlets
on American Writers, No. 38 (Minneapolis: University of Minnesota

Aiken's father was a Harvard-trained physician who practiced in Savannah. Aiken himself went to Harvard in the fall of 1907. Because of certain postponements and delays he received his degree in June 1912.[3]

When Aiken was eleven years old he experienced an event that changed the course of much of his later life. He discovered both parents dead, in what had evidently been both an act of murder and suicide. In *Ushant*, Aiken makes reference to the fact that this event established the course of his life. He began the search for "an equivalent that those two angelic people would have thought acceptable" *(Ushant*, p. 303). Aiken explains this idea as follows:

> And, of course, nothing could be more obvious than that thread, in the developing design of his life, that ever-increasing need for finding in his surroundings, and for making sure that it was there, the artifact of civilization, the artifact that was its sign manual. The finished forms and rituals of a fixed and conscious society, a society of fine lives in fine houses, in a social frame that was elaborate, finely elaborate—it was this that he had perpetually been searching for all his life. . . . And, paralleling this search for the civilized artifact, in all its forms, had been the unremitting quest for an equivalent

---

Press, 1964) , p. 6. One of the few biographical studies of Aiken is Houston Peterson's *The Melody of Chaos* (New York: Longmans, Green and Co., 1931) . This book primarily studies Aiken's work to 1930, though it includes biographical matter and letters received by the author from Aiken himself. Another book of interest here is Jay Martin, *Conrad Aiken, A Life of His Art* (Princeton: Princeton University Press, 1962) . Also, one can refer to a work of Aiken for some enlightenment about his life. See Conrad Aiken, *Ushant: An Essay* (New York and Boston: Duell, Sloan and Pearce, and Little, Brown and Company, 1952) . While this book is not an autobiography in the conventional sense, it is a record of Aiken's "stream-of-consciousness" memory, reminiscent in some ways of the poet's 1927 novel, *Blue Voyage*. In *Ushant*, however, a mature Conrad Aiken speculates about his life with keen insight.

3. It should be noted that the Harvard classes of 1910–1915 included such individuals as T. S. Eliot, John Reed, Walter Lippmann, E. E. Cummings, and Robert Benchley. Also, Aiken was chosen class poet during his senior year.

finesse and logic in understanding, a quest which had led him from Darwin to Nietzsche and Bergson, for instance, and Santayana, and from these in turn to Petrie and Freud. An ambiguous thread, a two-voiced theme: following simultaneously the precept of the parents to live as consciously as possible (as they themselves had done) but also to live as richly, and beautifully, as possible, as well. Would they have approved of the enormous English digression—if digression it was to turn out to be? At all events they would have understood the necessity for it, and for his there securing for himself, for the time being, at least, that fitness of environment which might be conducive to such "work" as he could ever find time for. (p. 303)

This quest to live as meaningfully as possible has certainly been a driving force in Aiken's life. It has meant the development of a keen awareness of self and a profound quest for identity. Henry Wells has explained Aiken and his work in these terms: "Along with relentless introspection in Aiken goes a profound melancholy, defeatism, and despair, such as only the romantic school has fostered."[4]

In another approach toward an understanding of Aiken and his work, Houston Peterson in *The Melody of Chaos* (1931) tries to decipher the difficulties of our times through the experience of the quest for identity as seen in the complexities of mental life. He believes that a morbid interest in the complexities of mental life arose as a result of the following complications:

(1) the scientific picture of the universe which has excluded God and forced man, frightened, back into himself.

(2) the mechanization of living and working condi-

---

4. *New Poets from Old: A Study in Literary Genetics* (New York: Columbia University Press, 1940), p. 293.

tions which brings about an excessive interest in the vast, consoling realm of revery.

(3) the undermining of our moral tradition and the consequent confusion of our whole mental outlook.

(4) the romantic movement with its emphasis on the inner life and more specifically the novel of minute analysis which has made us increasingly aware of our contradictory involved natures.

(5) psychology in its many-sided developments, which compels us to be complicated even when we want to be simple. (p. 17)

Romantic ideas, like all other ideas, are either being discarded or modified to fit the tenor of our times. In general, Aiken's later works show a broadening of his outlook; that is, they appear to be less romantic than his previous ones. This is not necessarily because of an essential change in basic views. Rather, it appears to be owing to a maturation enhanced by travel, wider reading, and more effective use of his powerful imagination. But "his two fundamental attitudes of pessimism and introspection are unchanged" (Wells, p. 294). And these attitudes have been primarily employed by Aiken in man's search for identity. Discussing one of Aiken's long poems, "The Kid" (1947), Roy Harvey Pearce caught the full impact of Aiken's involvement with the problem of identity:

> For—if a work which is so often tediously proliferating can ever fairly be reduced to its essentials—Aiken's essential theme is modern man's search for identity, which develops into a search for a means of discovering that identity, which in turn develops into a conviction that the seeking and what is sought are one. In the end that identity is proved to be a kind of non-identity, and man to be just another product of cosmic process. His power of discovery is an aspect of that process. For Aiken, language, bound up as it is in cosmic process,

cannot mean but rather can only evoke. It can evoke not an objective world but the process of making the world a subject and so of discovering the movement and power of the subjective.[5]

The whole concept of subjectivity and that of objectivity have been given powerful stimulation by such phenomena as dynamic psychology, the philosophical school of existentialism, and the scientific spirit of the twentieth century. All of these experiences did not happen in a vacuum, but were the outgrowth, as previously indicated, of many forces. Aiken is well-versed in literary history and understands full well the impact made upon it by modern depth psychology. Peterson sees Aiken in this regard as follows:

> Aiken has taken modern psychology seriously and immersed himself in its lore, with a poet's privileges. Some of his closest friends have been psychiatrists and he often wishes he had become one himself. An extreme introvert with a critical turn that is brutally objective, he is well qualified to understand cases of morbid repression, multiple personality and the whole literature of spiritual ambiguity. He has deliberately made this strange material the subject of his work, and may be considered the initiator of those long analytic poems which are among the most characteristic modes of contemporary verse. (*The Melody of Chaos*, pp. 18–19)

Discussing Aiken's *Preludes for Memnon* (1931), Joseph Warren Beach emphasizes the point that Aiken features "the moral terror" of men as they contemplate "the emptiness and futility of their lives."[6] And Beach believes that Aiken's insight into the meaninglessness of men's lives is of a telling nature. Beach writes:

5. *The Continuity of American Poetry* (Princeton: Princeton University Press, 1961), pp. 349–50.
6. *Obsessive Images: Symbolism in the Poetry of the 1930's and 1940's,* ed. William Van O'Connor (Minneapolis: University of Minnesota Press, 1960), pp. 62–69.

But it is abundantly clear that the revulsion recorded
by Aiken is not, as in other poets, against the evil in
men's hearts, their viciousness; that the sense of guilt
does not enter into this feeling; and that there is not the
faintest hint of what would ordinarily be considered
theological implications. (p. 62)

Aiken was among the first of the twentieth-century
American poets to bring about a fusion of subjective psychology and lyricism. Commenting on his work in this regard, George F. Whicher writes:

Two successive stages are observable in Aiken's poetry.
In half a dozen books from *Earth Triumphant* (1914)
to *The House of Dust* (1920) he experimented with
tenuous musical rhythms and with the formulation of
metaphysical and psychological ideas against a background of chaos. Beginning with *Punch: The Immortal
Liar* (1921) Aiken began a period of groping for symbols of frustration and arrested development, a search
which still continues without coming measurably nearer
to its goal. Though his *Selected Poems* (1929) were
awarded a Pulitzer Prize, Aiken's lyrical gift seems to
have fallen unripe. His prose, particularly in his short
stories, excels in the creation of uncanny mental atmos-
pheres. He has written a collection of trenchant critical
comments on contemporary poets in *Skepticisms* (1919)
and a notable essay on Emily Dickinson which forms the
preface to an admirable selection from her earliest published poems.[7]

Another critic offers additional insight in this regard
into Aiken's poetry. In a review of Aiken's *Selected Poems*
written during the thirties, George Dillon made the following observation:

---

7. "The Twentieth Century," in *The Literature of the American
People: An Historical and Critical Survey*, ed. Arthur Hobson Quinn
(New York: Appleton-Century-Crofts, Inc., 1951) , p. 867.

Conrad Aiken, perhaps more consistently than any other contemporary poet, has written in a form which is neither lyric nor narrative, but rather resembles what used to be called philosophical poetry. One may still call it that, I suppose; but in the instance of Mr. Aiken's long, loosely made poems (so different in everything but their length and looseness from familiar prototypes such as Wordsworth's *Prelude*) one is tempted to substitute the more modern term "psychological." At any rate, the mind that keeps its journal here could not have belonged to any century but this one. It is elaborately skeptical and honest, and not a little neurotic. It is continually pained and nonplused by the consciousness of its futility, and by the pursuit—through every *nuance* of sensation, thought, and metaphysical conjecture—of a "reality" it would be nonplused and pained to find.[8]

The tone of these remarks indicates an awareness of Aiken's poems having some connection with psychological underpinnings. Dillon believes that the poet's style has been influenced by T. S. Eliot, and like Eliot, Aiken "inhabits a waste-land of intellectual disillusion" (p. 222). But unlike Eliot, according to Dillon, Aiken is more compromising in his credo of despair. Speaking of this, Dillon says: "His biographies of defeated souls usually end on a note of hope or resignation" (p. 222). A good example of this is the first ten lines of "The Pilgrimage of Festus" from Aiken's *The Divine Pilgrim*.

And at last, having sacked in imagination many cities
And seen the smoke of them spread fantastically along
    the sky,
Having set foot upon so many walls, fallen and black-
    ened,

8. "Mr. Aiken's Poetry," *Poetry* 37 (January 1931): 221. One must keep in mind that at the time the above review was written, Freudian psychoanalysis had not reached the stage of widespread influence it achieved in later years.

And heard the harsh lamentations of women,
And watched without pity the old men, betraying their
        vileness,
Tear at their beards, and curse, and die,
Festus, coming alone to an eastern place
Of brown savannahs and wind-gnawed trees,
Climbed a rock that faced alone to the northward
And sat, and clasped his knees.[9]

Here, the protagonist is Festus. He is at an impasse.
Introspection, the feeling of being alone, and a sense of
resignation all come into place. Much of this, of course,
is the plight of modern man, and Dillon believes, as indicated above, that Aiken's poetry depicts this plight by ending either on a note of hope or resignation. In the final
lines of "The Pilgrimage of Festus," one is treated to the
concept of hope Aiken seems to enjoy:

Then Festus laughed, for he looked in his heart and saw
His worlds made young again,
And heard the sound of a many-people music,
And joyously into the world of himself set forward
Forgetting the long black aftermath of pain.
                                        (pp. 275–76)

The psychological factors involved in resignation and
hope are closely related to each other. One may resign
himself to his fate, hoping down deep that things will
change for the better; or, one may constantly live on a note
of hope, resigned to the fact that he is in a hopeless situation. Whatever characteristic may be in operation at any
one moment, Aiken believes that man's struggle is still to
a large degree an internal one, one in which man cannot
run away from his condition.

Henry Murray, a Freudian psychologist and psycho-

---

9. Conrad Aiken, *Collected Poems* (New York: Oxford University Press,
1953), p. 222. Unless otherwise indicated, all references to Aiken's poetry
will be from this volume.

analytically oriented critic, has explained this phenomenon regarding Aiken as follows:

"Man," says Proust, "is the creature who cannot get
outside himself, who knows others only in himself, and
when he says the contrary he lies." Aiken has never lied
by saying the contrary. He has never even *tried* to get
outside himself. At the very outset, it seems, he knew
his special fate: to follow the grain of his nature and
thereby to discover, in his own singular and undupli-
cated mind, the features of other inward turning minds.
Thus he is representative of a type. Going still farther
he arrived at those "wondrous depths," that Melville
reached, "where strange shapes of the unwarped primal
world glided to and fro before his passive yes." Thus
Aiken is universal. He belongs with those whose imagi-
nations are less invited by the world of social interactions
than by "the picture world which is ourselves," the
beauty and the horror mixed.[10]

It should be pointed out here that Murray's view of
Aiken is a positive one. He believes that the poet is involved in a continuous search in man's effort to answer
some basic questions about himself. Dillon, on the other
hand, appears to see this as a negative aspect of Aiken's
work. Dillon writes:

Except for a veil of romantic allegory which is always
sketchy and transparent, the reader is face to face with
the author *in propria persona*—an extremely introspec-
tive author holding an endless dialogue with himself.
It is a meditation in which question receives question in
reply; it goes on and on, and gets nowhere. . . . ("Mr.
Aiken's Poetry," p. 222)

Dillon, as can be inferred from the above quotation, is
not favorably disposed toward Aiken's work. The furthest
he will allow himself to look positively on Aiken's work, at

10. "Poet of Creative Dissolution," *Wake* 11 (1952): 100–101.

the time of writing (1931) , is to suggest that the poet is a young man of promise.

AIKEN'S CONCEPT OF BEAUTY AND AWARENESS AND HIS PSYCHOANALYTIC INSIGHTS INTO SELECTED POETRY

Conrad Aiken's view of life is a large one. It is vitally tied to his writings. "The aim that pervades all of Aiken's poetry and prose is perpetual extension of consciousness, perpetual discovery, and perpetual communication: to see everything—especially whatever the barriers of repression once concealed—, to embrace everything, and to express everything" (Murray, p. 103) .

This "perpetual extension of consciousness" also operates on a fundamental concept of aesthetics, according to Aiken. In one of his early articles on criticism,[11] Aiken discussed concepts of good and beauty in such terms as "moral beauty" and "aesthetic beauty." He believes that man's need for beauty is so great that he develops the field of art in order to satisfy this hunger. The reason for a deep involvement with beauty, according to Aiken, is found in the following consideration:

> And the real explanation will not be metaphysical but psychological. Let us rashly posit that the pleasurable feeling we know as "beauty" is simply, in essence, the profound satisfaction we feel when, through the medium of fantasy, we escape from imposed limitations into an aggrandized personality and a harmonized universe. This kind of satisfaction not only can be said to give rise to the feeling "beauty"—it *is* beauty. Its very essence is illusion. And illusion is vital to us because of the re-

11. "A Basis for Criticism," *The New Republic* 34 (April 1923) , part 2: 1–6.

strictions, of every kind, that hem us in: we come into
the world confident of omnipotence, and daily our power
dwindles. Brightness falls from the air, pain teaches us
that we are mortal, injury leaves us crippled, knowledge serves rather to show us our weakness than our
strength. We look back to that earlier hour as to something infinitely bright and happy, we desire passionately
and constantly to return to it, and we seek in day-dream
to do so. It has been urged that in the day-dream, or
art, we do not really seek to escape from ourselves, but,
precisely, to find ourselves. But what part of ourselves
is it that we find? Is it not exactly that part of us which
has been wounded and would be made whole: that part
of us which desires wings and has none, longs for immortality and knows that it must die, craves unlimited
power and has instead "common sense" and the small
bitter "actual": that part of us, in short, which is im-
prisoned and would escape? . . . There can be little
question about it, and it is precisely of the associations
connected with these major psychic frustrations that
we have evolved the universal language of healing which
we call art. Let us not hastily condemn this view simply
because it savors of the often-flouted "new" psychology.
Freud is not, by two thousand two hundred years, the
first to see art as primarily a process of wish-fulfillment.
Let us recall Aristotle's theory of katharsis, and rub our
eyes. The difference between katharsis and wish-fulfillment is slight to the point of disappearance. ("A Basis
for Criticism," p. 4)

Perhaps the above explanation also indicates something
about Aiken's special relationship with the field of psycho-
analysis. To a large extent, Freud was the arch-realist who
was not afraid of facing up to the dark side of life, even
when beauty was in his immediate experience. Aiken too
has confronted darkness with his unique literary ability,
but has not succumbed to a decided pessimistic outlook.
Hence, Aiken took to Freud's beliefs, not for the purpose
of finding a resting place of intellectual certitude, but

rather as a labyrinthine experience which one has to en-
counter and work through in order to grow intellectually
and emotionally. Not all poets were able to do this. Murray captures the importance of this experience as follows:

> Some poets, sensing its lethal potencies, shunned psy-
> choanalysis completely. Others took a look at it, shied
> away like a nervous horse. Some nibbled at it. A few
> were victimized. Almost alone in his generation Aiken
> proved equal to the peril. He allowed the Freudian
> dragon to swallow him, and then, after a sufficient so-
> journ in its maw, cut his way out to a new freedom.
> When he emerged he was stocked with the lore of psy-
> choanalysis but neither subjugated nor impeded by it.
> Aiken and Freud were, in a profound sense, fellow-
> spirits—something which the younger man recognized in
> college, but which the master did not suspect until much
> later while reading Aiken's subtle *Great Circle*. On the
> strength of this book (not *King Coffin,* my favorite)
> Freud offered the poet a three-months' analysis as a free
> experiment. Unfortunately this opportunity could not
> be accepted. The two men never met. ("Poet of Creative
> Dissolution," pp. 101–102)

The manner in which Aiken was able to experience his
relationship with depth psychology, notably psychoanalysis, is in all probability owing to another important aspect
of his background. He does not appear to be one of those
imaginative individuals who are geared to reversing the
course of modern science. Nowhere does he blame people
like Marx, Darwin, and Freud for depriving twentieth-century man of his illusion of greatness or omnipotence. Those
who do are described in the words of Alfred Kazin as follows: "These people are hopeless, yet there is one element
of tragic truth in their indictment of the modern spirit:
more and more people lack the sense of tradition with

which to assimilate the endless shocks and changes of the twentieth century."[12] Conrad Aiken is certainly not of that vintage.[13] Aiken's literary and historical sense of tradition provided him with a necessary sense of balance as he approached the field of psychoanalysis. Frederick J. Hoffman explains this as follows:

> He was not unaware of the abuses which psychoanalysis might suffer, or of the imperfect grasp which the amateur might have of it. The psychoanalyst plays an ambiguous role in his fiction. With all due respect to the seriousness of studies in the new psychology, Aiken presents a normal resistance against its attempts to resolve all modern dilemmas with the magic of words and the suave, smooth domination of the analyst over the tragic circumstances of the modern soul. Like many another artist of his time, Aiken, captivated by the new vision of the human soul, is reluctant to leave its horrors and fascinations for the cold, clear, reasonable light of the analyst who usually points to the status quo and bids the patient find in it a sensible solution of his problems.[14]

---

12. "Psychoanalysis and Literary Culture Today," in Hendrik M. Ruitenbeek, ed. *Psychoanalysis and Literature* (New York: E. P. Dutton & Co., Inc., 1964), p. 10.

13. Aiken's experience as a novelist is also of interest in this context. One critic observes: "Most conspicuously indebted to Joyce among American novelists was Conrad Aiken. 'I decided very early,' Aiken said in a reply to a questionnaire (*New Verse*, 1934), 'that Freud, and his coworkers and rivals and followers, were making the most important contribution of the century to the understanding of man and his consciousness; accordingly I made it my business to learn as much from them as I could.' *Great Circle* (1933), *King Coffin* (1935), and *Blue Voyage* (1927) all testify to Aiken's interest in Joyce and his concern over the Freudian explanation of the human consciousness." See Frederick J. Hoffman, *The 20's: American Writing in the Postwar Decade*, 2d ed. (New York: The Free Press, 1962), p. 246.

14. *Freudianism and the Literary Mind*, 2d ed. (Baton Rouge: Louisiana State University Press, 1957), p. 275. Hoffman also tells us that Aiken learned from a Dr. G. P. McCouch of Cambridge, a psychiatrist friend, "about the subversive doctrines of Professor Sigmund Freud." In a letter to Hoffman, Aiken dates his first acquaintance with Freudianism "about 1909 or 1910" (pp. 274–75).

The problem of evaluating any poet's work is definitely involved with growth in craft and theme. Aiken's work is no exception. However, the problem of evaluation in this sense is often made more complicated by extraneous reasons. As regards Aiken, Hoffman points out the following:

> Even from a point some forty-eight years after his first publication, it is difficult to evaluate a man's poetry when there is such a rich profusion of it. Since 1914 (the year of *Earth Triumphant*) , Conrad Aiken has published a total of twenty-nine volumes of poems: these include the *Selected Poems* of 1929 (for which, in 1930, he received the Pulitzer Prize) , the *Collected Poems* of 1953, and the recent edition of *Selected Poems* (1961) . Certain other volumes are reprintings or rearrangements of poems previously published. The 1949 publication of *The Divine Pilgrim* by the University of Georgia Press is an example: in it all of the "Symphonies," from the *Charnel Rose* to "Changing Mind," are reordered, some of them much revised, and equipped with prefaces and explanations. But the majority of the volumes are fresh, new, original poems, which add steadily to the reputation of the poet.[15]

It is fitting to make these general observations about Aiken's poetry. In the beginning there was the usual experience of imitation. This was followed by an avalanche of ideas and forms; the poetry being written could not take appropriate advantage of this acceleration. This was followed by a period in which there was a serious attempt made at formulating independent philosophies and modes of thematic structures and rhythms. Then there were two years of integration, where refinement and close scrutiny were the characteristics of the poet's development. In Aiken's case, whatever experimentation followed was not

---

15. *Conrad Aiken* (New York: Twayne Publishers, Inc., 1962) , p. 69.

in the direction of going to extremes for the sake of such an experience. He was, and still remains, a "gifted traditionalist." Hoffman writes: "Rather, his development has been toward a modern restatement of traditional manners" (*Conrad Aiken,* p. 71). In this development, Freudian psychoanalytic thought appears to have been helpful to Aiken.

From a psychoanalytic standpoint, Aiken's "autobiographical" study, *Ushant,* has been criticized for various reasons by David Rein.[16] He believes that Aiken makes extraordinary attempts at self-revelation, including a series of interpretations of his own life in terms of Freud's theories of his oedipal theme. Rein says:

> Aiken's psychoanalytic interpretations are not supported by enough evidence to be really persuasive. With all its shortcomings, however, the book is a considerable effort. (p. 410)

Then proceeding to regard Aiken's entire output, including his poetry, Rein continues:

> That, it seems to me, is the best way to rate Aiken's work as a whole: a considerable effort. In his fiction and in his autobiography he has recounted his adult maladjustments with an extraordinary passion for understanding himself and, guided by psychoanalytic knowledge, with some exceptional insights. His failures, it is true, occupy the larger part of his output. But most of the time he has been trying to conquer new territory for literature, and his successes, particularly in his better short stories, are works of beauty, blending in novel ways the psychoanalyst's knowledge with the poet's skill. (p. 410)

---

16. See David M. Rein, "Conrad Aiken and Psychoanalysis," *The Psychoanalytic Review* 42 (1955): 409–10.

Aiken's interest in psychoanalysis was discussed in one of his earliest works.[17] He writes that "poetry, like the dream, is an outcome of suppression, a release of complexes" (p. 33). He then proceeds to discuss what he believes happens during the period of poetic composition. Included in his discussion are references to the conscious, subconscious, and unconscious. He sees the poet as both "patient" and "analyst" in the sense that the poet is "a curious blending" of the two (pp. 102–3).

Aiken's *The Divine Pilgrim* is a long poem divided into six parts. These are: "The Charnel Rose," "The Jig of Forslin," "The House of Dust," "Senlin: A Biography," and part of "The Pilgrimage of Festus," and "Changing Mind." Originally, most of the parts were published as separate works. With some revisions they were published in 1949 as one under the above title. Rein briefly discusses the poem, and his remarks can easily be summarized. "The Charnel Rose" is not clearly meaningful enough from a psychoanalytical point of view. There is a chorus of voices and influences at work here that obscures the reality of a more specific purpose operating. Aiken's work in this poem is too disjointed.[18]

"The Jig of Forslin," the second poem in the series, is supposed to have a special theme, according to its preface. "This theme is the process of vicarious wish fulfillment by which civilized man enriches his circumscribed life and

---

17. Conrad Aiken, *Scepticisms: Notes on Contemporary Poetry* (New York: Alfred A. Knopf, 1919). Aiken also acknowledges a direct influence of psychoanalysis on one of his poems as follows: "For the poem 'Hallowe'en' in this volume, I am very greatly indebted to Dr. Richard Sterba, from whose beautiful article on the ritual origins and psychoanalytical implications of Hallowe'en, in *The American Imago* for November 1948, I have drawn not only part of my theme but images and phrases as well." Conrad Aiken, *Sheepfold Hill: Fifteen Poems* (New York: Sagamore Press, 1958), p. 5.

18. "Conrad Aiken and Psychoanalysis," pp. 403–4.

obtains emotional balance."[19] While Rein believes "Forslin" does depict a series of vicarious experiences, the poem lacks an essential unifying personality. He further believes that the term *man* is too tenuous here and does not come through psychologically, insofar as psychoanalysis is concerned. And according to Rein, the entire poem suffers from a lack of specificity, which the discipline of psychoanalysis could not tolerate (pp. 403–4).

In an early review of Aiken's *Selected Poems,* R. P. Blackmur made the following statement:

Mr. Aiken has not actually changed a jot. Merely his later poems have substituted one set of accents for another. As it happens, most people today prefer the harsh, precisely suggestive, psychological poetry he is now writing to the earlier lyrical, vaguely suggestive pieces. It is a matter of taste, and amounts to liking fifty pages better than three hundred. But the taste may be wrong and may be corrected. . . .[20]

The point is that each poet has a right to deal with his subject as he sees fit. And taste, to a large extent, still depends upon time, place, situation, and the individual reader's preference. It seems to me that a poet like Aiken may be equipped with both psychological lore and lyrical acumen, as is evidenced in the fourth section of Aiken's poem, "Electra":

19. *Collected Poems,* p. 866. It is interesting to note that in a review of Houston Peterson's *The Melody of Chaos,* reference is made to the fact that one of the reasons why Peterson is unkind to T. S. Eliot is that "The Jig of Forslin" anticipated "The Wasteland," which Peterson feels does not have priority over Aiken's poem. See Allan Tate, "The Author of 'John Deth,'" *The New Republic* 67 (July 22, 1931): 265–66. Further discussion regarding Aiken and Eliot can be found in Joseph Warren Beach, "Conrad Aiken and T. S. Eliot: Echoes and Overtones," *PMLA* 69 (September 1954): 753–62.

20. "Conrad Aiken," *The New Republic* 61 (January 22, 1930): 256.

'Under this water-lily knee' (she said)
'Blood intricately flows, corpuscle creeps,
The white like sliced cucumber, and the red
Like poker-chip! Along dark mains they flow
As wafts the sponging heart. The water-lily,
Subtle in seeming, bland to lover's hand
Upthrust exploring, is in essence gross,
Multiple and corrupt. Thus, in the moonlight'
 (She hooked a curtain and disclosed the moon)
'How cold and lucent! And this naked breast,
Whereon a blue vein writes Diana's secret,
How simple! How seductive of the palm
That flatters with the finest tact of flesh!
Not silver is this flank, nor ivory,
Gold it is not, not copper, but distilled
Of lust in moonlight, and my own hand strays
To touch it in this moonlight, whence it came.'
Naked in moonlight, like a doll of wax,
On the stone floor nocturnal, she stood still
But moved her hands. The cruel mouth was curved,
Smiling a little; and her eyes were fixed,
In wonder, on Diana's hieroglyph.
And it was then (her nineteenth autumn come)
She heard at last, so often prophesied,
The singing of the blood. Her beauty broke
To sound beneath her hands, which moved from breast
To knee and back again, and bruised the flank
That was not gold or copper, but became
A throbbing sound beneath palpating palms.
Thus stood awhile; then sighed; then dropped her hands
And wept, as he (who loved her) had foretold.[21]

Here, in the above lines, we have what appears to be many ingredients of basic Freudian dynamics, couched in lyrical tones.

In Freudian psychoanalytic theory, one usually starts with the obvious and works backward in order to gain a de-

---

21. *Collected Poems*, pp. 466–67.

velopmental view of what has happened in a particular instance. Always, the psychoanalytically oriented researcher includes as part of his knowledge an awareness of denial and annihilation, and awareness that the beginning of life means a direction toward an end. Between these points of life and death there is consciousness, with all its ramifications of the unconscious; and knowledge, which awareness implies often creates a responsibility and a real predicament. In a review of Aiken's *The Coming Forth by Day of Osiris Jones* and *Preludes for Memnon,* Blackmur has stated:

> More interesting is the predicament of the consciousness that knows. Consciousness seems always to stop short of its object, and is defined by its limitations. There is a gap, a chasm, all around it, which is the gap between what we know and our knowing. As our knowing shifts, grows, diminishes—as we know more or differently or know that we know less—we proceed through disillusion. Knowledge is the terrible key to that ignorance in which, if we turn the key, we shall lock ourselves; and there is no unlocking. Yet a mind may not use its ignorance; ignorance is a condition to be achieved, like grace, and is not a weapon; the weapon is knowledge, a sharpening, a definition, of the fragments of consciousness. The pursuit is full of victory and assertion; the most formidable sensations are vanquished. The end is denial and annihilation; the abyss surveyed by consciousness widens, consciousness topples and is engulfed. In our ends are our beginnings. Between-times we are conscious of more or less.[22]

Freud has made it clear that the human species must essentially deal with the kind of consciousness Aiken is referring to if it is to survive. "Men have gained control over the forces of nature to such an extent that with their

---

22. "The Day Before the Daybreak," *Poetry* 40 (April 1932) : 41.

help they would have no difficulty in exterminating one another to the last man."[23]

The ever-widening consciousness that Aiken speaks of includes an awareness of reality and a facing up to its implications. Hence, in the opening seventeen lines of the *Preludes for Memnon* we read:

> Winter for a moment takes the mind; the snow
> Falls past the arclight; icicles guard a wall;
> The wind moans through a crack in the window;
> A keen sparkle of frost is on the sill.
> Only for a moment; as spring too might engage it,
> With a single crocus in the loam, or a.pair of birds;
> Or summer with hot grass; or autumn with a yellow
>   leaf.
> Winter is there, outside, is here in me:
> Drapes the planets with snow, deepens the ice on the
>   moon,
> Darkens the darkness that was already darkness.
> The mind too has its snows, its slippery paths,
> Walls bayonetted with ice, leaves ice-encased.
> Here is the in-drawn room, to which you return
> When the wind blows from Arcturus: here is the fire
> At which you warm your hands and glaze your eyes;
> The piano, on which you touch the cold treble;
> Five notes like breaking icicles; and then silence.[24]

In her joint review of *The Coming Forth by Day of Osiris Jones* and the *Preludes for Memnon,* Marianne Moore observes of the former:

> In *The Coming Forth by Day of Osiris Jones,* which is psychorealistic poetic drama intentionally distorted, the arrangement is that of the disrelated chapters of a funerary roll or grave book; and as on a late dynastic

---

23. *Civilization and Its Discontents,* ed. and trans. James Strachey (New York: W. W. Norton & Co., Inc., 1961) , p. 92.
24. *Collected Poems,* p. 498.

roll or on one of the Empire there were sometimes illus-
trations, there arise here—not consecutively—favorite
thoughts or might one say vignettes, and certain sensa-
tions prominent to the consciousness of Osiris Jones.[25]

The consciousness of Osiris is quite real. Freudian
"pessimism" based on how things really are comes out in
the opening lines of *The Coming Forth by Day of Osiris
Jones:*

> It is a shabby backdrop of bright stars:
> one of the small interstices of time:
> the worn out north star northward, and Orion
> to westward spread in ruined light. Eastward,
> the other stars disposed,—or indisposed;—
> x-ward or y-ward, the sick sun inflamed;
> and all his drunken planets growing pale.
> We watch them, and our watching is this hour.
>   (p. 574)

In a telling analysis of certain poems of Aiken and a
plea for him as a major poet and force in poetry, Rufus A.
Blanshard stated in his concluding remarks:

> These notes for a survey must conclude with less atten-
> tion to the late poetry than it deserves. Although it
> maintains and refines the qualities that have already
> been noted in the two books of *Preludes* . . . Aiken has
> worked the theme of the double frontier, outer and in-
> ner, which constitutes for him the essence of American
> individualism and the key to his own past. Like *Ushant,*
> this poetry spirals out from intensely personal, and at
> the same time serenely objectified, experience.[26]

The "outer" and "inner" as mentioned in Blanshard's

25. "If A Man Die," *Hound & Horn* 5 (January-March 1932): 314.
This is also reprinted with slight changes in *Wake* 11 (1952): 50–56.
26. "Pilgrim's Progress: Conrad Aiken's Poetry," *Texas Quarterly* 1
(Winter 1958): 147.

review are essentially what depth psychology concerns itself with in terms of understanding human behavior.[27]

In Aiken's poem "Time in the Rock or Preludes to Definition," the third stanza of Part II, lines 14–18, reads:

Give us this day our daily death, that we may learn to live;
teach us that we trespass; that we may learn,
in wisdom, not in kindness, to forgive;
and in the granite of our own bones seal us daily.[28]

These lines express what such psychoanalytically oriented critics as Rein, Hoffman, Murray, Kazin, and others have been implying or suggesting about Aiken and his poetry; that he is an arch-realist who knows that life must be faced at all levels; that Conrad Aiken is fully aware that the art of birth involves the wisdom of facing death, in effect, living wisely.

What we have in Aiken's poetry then is an awareness (1) of inner and outer factors of personality, (2) of consciousness and unconsciousness, (3) of learning and wisdom from one's handling of reality, and (4) of the limitations of the human condition because of the ever-present possibility of death. One may say that Aiken's psychology as revealed in his poetry is not one of pessimism; rather, it is one of healthy skepticism and creative hopefulness.[29]

---

27. It is true that Freud was primarily concerned with internal aspects of personality; since his day, however, the newer concepts at work in psychoanalysis include the environment as a prime factor in man's psychological and sociological makeup. We need only to refer to Fromm, Horney, Adler, Sullivan, Jung, and the various schools of existential psychology.

28. *Collected Poems*, p. 666.

29. For more of Aiken's views on poets, poetry influences and depth psychology, see Robert Hunter Wilbur, "The Art of Poetry IX: Conrad Aiken—An Interview," *Paris Review* 11, no. 42 (Winter–Spring 1968) : 97–124. Also, see John K. Hutchens, "One Thing and Another," *Saturday Review* (December 20, 1969), pp. 24–25. The latter interview took place following Mr. Aiken's receipt of the 1969 National Book Committee's fifth National Medal for Literature.

Aiken remains a poet; he is not a trained psychologist. He has taken from Freud whatever he felt would help him in his endeavors. He has not tried to be a blind adherent or a compulsive antagonist of Freud or of any of the later developments in psychoanalysis. He has maintained a balanced attitude and utilized whatever insights he could gain from Freud to enhance his work as a poet.

5
Conclusion

A technical discussion of the differences between "schools" of psychoanalysis has not been of prime concern here. Poetry is a genre that appeals to all schools of modern depth psychology. The literary critic employing psychoanalytic tools in his understanding of poetry should be versed in psychoanalytic theory as well as in his knowledge of poetry. This kind of efficiency goes a long way in preventing the psychoanalytically oriented critic from going beyond the realm of his competence. This warning of course points to the fact that the psychoanalytically oriented literary critic should understand and closely follow trends in both psychoanalysis and literature.[1]

Freud's theories have been employed in literary criticism to explain the origin of individual poems and of poetry in general, and to interpret the particular work in question. Jung's theories of psychoanalysis have also lent

---

1. In terms of psychoanalysis and literary criticism the following has been observed: "As might be imagined, the various schools of psychoanalysis that come after Freud have, in changing his doctrines, changed psychoanalytic literary criticism. For example the followers of Adler substituted the inferiority and superiority complexes as the key to literary character analysis. Those who held to the teachings of Jung preferred to emphasize the collective unconscious of the race as revealed in the character, an unconscious which contained mystic elements. The tendency in more recent psychoanalytical criticism is to borrow concepts from all these schools, an eclecticism that parallels the eclecticism of many practicing psychoanalysts." Vernon Hall, Jr., *A Short History of Literary Criticism* (New York: New York University Press, 1963), p. 160.

themselves to the interpretative side of literature as well as to an evaluative approach. Since the task of the literary critic is to provide a wider consideration of the work under scrutiny, he can draw upon many fields for further illumination. And psychoanalysis is one of these fields from which the literary critic may profitably draw.

This exploratory study of selected psychoanalytically oriented criticism of selected poetry of Poe, Whitman, and Aiken should help point up the value and limitation of such criticism in the genre of poetry. This is especially the case if the critic keeps several facts in mind.

First, Poe, Whitman, and Aiken, like poets of all time, deal with such themes as birth, life, death, love, beauty, faith, hope, fear, anxiety, and many other human emotions and experiences. Second, each of the three poets is working within a particular tradition.

Poe writes within a romantic tradition made familiar by Byron, Keats, Shelley, Hugo, Heine, Leopardi, Lermontov, and others. It may be said he stepped into the tidal wave of the romantic movement after it had already established itself in Europe and was beginning to make itself felt in American literature. Whitman vaunts the rising exuberance of a growing America as he sings of himself with complete abandon and freedom. There is a deep biblical strain in Whitman, particularly reminiscent of Hebrew poetry as found in the *Old Testament*. And Conrad Aiken's poetry seems to be in a constant state of striving toward perfect symphonic arrangement; he aims to bring a closer relationship between poetry and music, very much in the tradition of the Greek playwrights. And as he concerns himself with conscious and unconscious elements of human thought, Aiken finds himself employing psychoanalytic insights in his poetry.

Hence, whatever psychoanalytically oriented school of

criticism focuses on the work of the poets under consideration, Poe, Whitman, and Aiken are still to be thought of as working both within their own frames of reference and within a larger poetic tradition.

Based on the information I have presented in the preceding chapters, I would conclude that in the consideration of poetry, psychoanalytic theory must not be grafted onto a poem for the purpose of proving its own validity. Rather, psychoanalytic theory may be skillfully employed by the critic as a means of presenting a widened understanding of a poem. I would also emphasize that the same holds true where the critic concerns himself with the poet's life by means of the poem, in order to understand the latter more fully.

This exploratory study indicates that psychoanalytically oriented criticism of poetry employs one or more of the following psychoanalytic considerations: (1) unconscious mental processes, (2) ego psychology, (3) defense mechanisms such as repression, resistance, identification, introjection, displacement, sublimation, and the like, (4) daydreaming, dreams, and dream interpretation, (5) the psychoanalytic concept of sexuality and/or the Oedipal theme, and (6) the concepts of omnipotence, pleasure and reality principles.

Interestingly enough, the life of each of the three poets—Poe, Whitman, and Aiken—conveniently lends itself to psychoanalytic interpretation. This places a special responsibility upon the psychoanalytically oriented critic of poetry. An interpretation of the life of a poet may or may not have something to do with a particular poem. The important thing at this point is the understanding of the poem, interesting though the individual life may be.

It may also be possible to arrive at a psychoanalytic interpretation of a poem without necessarily being acquainted with psychoanalytic theory. However, those who do have a knowledge of such theory obviously tend to be more sophisticated in their application of psychoanalytically oriented criticism than those who do not.

Finally, of the three poets, only Aiken had a conscious awareness of an interest in the field of psychoanalysis. This of course often revealed itself in his criticism and literary work. Nevertheless, while Poe and Whitman were not so sophisticated, their poems do deal with themes that lend themselves to psychoanalytic criticism.

Bibliography

Adler, Alfred. *The Practice and Theory of Individual Psychology,* trans. P. Radin. London: K. Paul, Trench, Trubner & Co., Ltd., 1946.

———. *What Life Should Mean to You,* ed. Alan Porter. Boston: Little, Brown and Company, 1931.

Adler, Kurt A., and Deutsch, Danica, eds. *Essays in Individual Psychology: Contemporary Application of Alfred Adler's Theories.* New York: Grove Press, Inc., 1959.

Aiken, Conrad. "A Basis for Criticism," *The New Republic* 34, pt. 2 (April 1923) : 1–6.

———. *A Reviewer's ABC: Collected Criticism,* ed. Rufus A. Blanshard. New York: Meridian Books, Inc., 1958.

———. *Blue Voyage.* New York: Charles Scribner's Sons, 1927.

———. *Collected Poems.* New York: Oxford University Press, 1953.

———. *The Coming Forth by Day of Osiris Jones.* New York: Charles Scribner's Sons, 1931.

———. *The Divine Pilgrim.* Athens: University of Georgia Press, 1949.

———. *Earth Triumphant and Other Tales in Verse.* New York: The Macmillan Company, 1914.

———. *Great Circle.* New York: Charles Scribner's Sons, 1933.

———. *The House of Dust: A Symphony.* Boston: The Four Seas Company, 1920.

———. *King Coffin.* New York: Charles Scribner's Sons, 1935.

———. *Preludes for Memnon.* New York: Charles Scribner's Sons, 1931.

———. *Punch: The Immortal Liar, Documents in His History.* New York: Alfred A. Knopf, Inc., 1921.

———. *Scepticisms: Notes on Contemporary Poetry.* New York: Alfred A. Knopf, Inc., 1919.

————. *Selected Poems.* New York: Charles Scribner's Sons, 1929.

————. *Sheepfold Hill: Fifteen Poems.* New York: Sagamore Press, 1958.

————. *Ushant: An Essay.* New York and Boston. Duell, Sloan and Pearce, and Little, Brown and Company, 1952.

Allen, Evie Allison. "A Check List of Whitman Publications 1945–1960," in Gay Wilson Allen, *Walt Whitman as Man, Poet, and Legend.* Carbondale: Southern Illinois University Press, 1961. Pp. 179–244.

Allen, Gay Wilson. *Walt Whitman as Man, Poet, and Legend.* Carbondale: Southern Illinois University Press, 1961.

————. *Walt Whitman Handbook.* Chicago: Packard and Company, 1946.

Allen, Hervey. *Israfel: The Life and Times of Edgar Allan Poe.* New York: Farrar & Rinehart, Inc., 1934.

Ansbacher, Heinz L. and Rowena R., eds. *The Individual Psychology of Alfred Adler.* New York: Basic Books, Inc., 1956.

Beach, Joseph Warren. "Conrad Aiken and T. S. Eliot: Echoes and Overtones," *PMLA* 69 (September 1954) : 753–62.

————. *Obsessive Images: Symbolism in the Poetry of the 1930's and 1940's,* ed. William Van O'Connor. Minneapolis: University of Minnesota Press, 1960.

Bergler, Edmund. *The Writer and Psychoanalysis.* Garden City, N.Y.: Doubleday & Company, Inc., 1950.

Blackmur, R. P. "Conrad Aiken," *The New Republic* 61 (January 22, 1930) : 255–56.

————. "The Day Before the Daybreak," *Poetry* 40 (April 1932): 39–44.

Blanshard, Rufus A. "Pilgrim's Progress: Conrad Aiken's Poetry," *Texas Quarterly* 1 (Winter 1958) : 135–48.

Bonaparte, Marie. *The Life and Works of Edgar Allan Poe: A Psycho-Analytic Interpretation,* trans. John Rodker. London: Imago Publishing Co. Ltd., 1949.

————. "Poe and the Function of Literature," in *Art and Psychoanalysis,* ed. William Phillips. Cleveland: The World Publishing Company, 1963. Pp. 54–88.

Briggs, Arthur E. *Walt Whitman: Thinker and Artist.* New York: Philosophical Library, 1952.

Brill, A. A. "The Introduction of Freud's Work in the United States," *American Journal of Sociology* 45 (1939) : 318–25.
———. "Poetry as an Oral Outlet," *The Psychoanalytical Review* 18 (October 1931) : 357–78.
Buranelli, Vincent. *Edgar Allan Poe.* New York: Twayne Publishers, Inc., 1961.
Burke, Kenneth. "Freud—and the Analysis of Poetry," *American Journal of Sociology* 45 (1939) : 391–417.
———. "Freud—and the Analysis of Poetry," in *Psychoanalysis and Literature,* ed. Hendrik M. Ruitenbeek. New York: E. P. Dutton & Co., Inc., 1964. Pp. 114–41.
Bychowski, Gustav. "Walt Whitman: A Study in Sublimation," in *Psychoanalysis and the Social Sciences,* ed. Géza Róheim. New York: International Universities Press, Inc., 1951. Vol. 3, 223–61.
Campbell, Killis. *The Mind of Poe and Other Studies.* Cambridge: Harvard University Press, 1933.
Canby, Henry Seidel. *Walt Whitman an American.* Boston: Houghton Mifflin Co., 1943.
Catel, Jean. *Walt Whitman: La Naissance du Poète.* Paris: Les Editions Rieder, 1929.
Chase, Richard. *Walt Whitman.* Minneapolis: University of Minnesota Press, 1961.
———. *Walt Whitman Reconsidered.* New York: William Sloane Associates, Inc., 1955.
Denney, Reuel. *Conrad Aiken.* University of Minnesota Pamphlets on American Writers, no. 38. Minneapolis: University of Minnesota Press, 1964.
de Selincourt, Ernest. *Wordsworthian and Other Studies.* New York: Russell & Russell, Inc., 1964.
Dillon, George. "Mr. Aiken's Poetry," *Poetry* 37 (January 1931) : 221–25.
Edel, Leon. "Notes on the Use of Psychological Tools in Literary Scholarship," *Literature and Psychology* 1 (September 1951) : 1–3.
Fodor, Nandor, and Frank Gaynor, eds. *Freud: Dictionary of Psychoanalysis.* New York: The Philosophical Library, Inc., 1950.
Foerster, Norman. *American Criticism: A Study in Literary*

Theory from Poe to the Present. New York: Russell & Russell, Inc., 1962.

Fraiberg, Louis. *Psychoanalysis & American Literary Criticism.* Detroit: Wayne State University Press, 1960.

Freud, Sigmund. *Beyond the Pleasure Principle, Group Psychology, and Other Works.* Vol. 18 of *The Standard Edition of the Complete Psychological Works of Sigmund Freud,* rev. and ed. James Strachey. London: The Hogarth Press and the Institute of Psycho-Analysis, 1955.

————. *Civilization and Its Discontents,* ed. and trans. James Strachey. New York: W. W. Norton & Company, Inc., 1961.

————. "Creative Writers and Day-Dreaming," *Jensen's 'Gradiva' and Other Works.* Vol. 9 (1906–1908) of *The Standard Edition of the Complete Psychological Works of Sigmund Freud,* rev. and ed. James Strachey. London: The Hogarth Press and the Institute of Psycho-Analysis, 1959. Pp. 143–53.

————. *A General Introduction to Psychoanalysis,* trans. Joan Riviere. Garden City, N.Y.: Garden City Publishing Company, Inc., 1943.

————. *Group Psychology and the Analysis of the Ego,* trans. James Strachey. London: The Hogarth Press and the Institute of Psycho-Analysis, 1948.

————. "History of the Psychoanalytic Movement," in *The Basic Writings of Sigmund Freud,* trans. and ed. A. A. Brill. New York: Random House, Inc., 1938. Pp. 946–58.

————. "The Interpretation of Dreams," in *The Basic Writings of Sigmund Freud,* trans. and ed. A. A. Brill. New York: Random House, Inc., 1938. Pp. 181–549.

————. *The Interpretation of Dreams* I. Vol. 4 (1900) of *The Standard Edition of the Complete Psychological Works of Sigmund Freud,* rev. and ed. James Strachey. London: The Hogarth Press and the Institute of Psycho-Analysis, 1953.

————. *The Interpretation of Dreams* II, and *On Dreams.* Vol. 5 (1900–1901) of *The Standard Edition of the Complete Psychological Works of Sigmund Freud,* rev. and ed. James Strachey. London: The Hogarth Press and the Institute of Psycho-Analysis, 1953.

————. *Leonardo da Vinci: A Psycho-Sexual Study of an*

Infantile Reminiscence, trans. A. A. Brill. New York: Random House, Inc., 1947.

————. *Moses and Monotheism,* trans. Katherine Jones. New York: Vintage Books, Inc., 1955.

————. *New Introductory Lectures on Psycho-Analysis,* trans. W. J. H. Sprott. New York: W. W. Norton & Company, Inc., 1933.

————. "On the History of the Psycho-Analytic Movement," in *Early Papers and History of the Psycho-Analytical Movement.* Vol. 1 of *Collected Papers,* trans. Joan Riviere. The International Psycho-Analytical Library, ed. Ernest Jones, no. 7. London: The Hogarth Press and the Institute of Psycho-Analysis, 1949. Pp. 287–359.

————. "On the History of the Psycho-Analytic Movement," *On the History of the Psycho-Analytic Movement; Papers on Metapsychology; and Other Works.* Vol. 14 (1914–1916) of *The Standard Edition of the Complete Psychological Works of Sigmund Freud,* rev. and ed. James Strachey. London: The Hogarth Press and the Institute of Psycho-Analysis, 1957. Pp. 7–66.

————. "Origin and Development of Psychoanalysis," trans. Harry W. Chase. *American Journal of Psychology* 21 (April 1910) : 181–218.

————. *The Problem of Anxiety,* trans. H. A. Bunker. New York: The Psychoanalytic Quarterly Press and W. W. Norton & Company, Inc., 1936.

————. "Psycho-Analysis," *Beyond the Pleasure Principle, Group Psychology and Other Works.* Vol. 18 (1920–1922) of *The Standard Edition of the Complete Psychological Works of Sigmund Freud,* rev. and ed. James Strachey. London: The Hogarth Press and the Institute of Psycho-Analysis, 1955. Pp. 235–54.

————. "Psycho-Analysis," *Miscellaneous Papers, 1888–1938.* Vol. 5 of *Collected Papers,* ed. James Strachey. The International Psycho-Analytical Library, ed. Ernest Jones, no. 37. London: The Hogarth Press and the Institute of Psycho-Analysis, 1950. Pp. 107–30.

————. "The Question of a *Weltanschauung,*" *New Introductory Lectures on Psycho-Analysis and Other Works.* Vol. 22 (1932–1936) of *The Standard Edition of the Com-*

plete Psychological Works of Sigmund Freud, rev. and ed. James Strachey. London: The Hogarth Press and the Institute of Psycho-Analysis, 1964. Pp. 158–82.

————. "The Relation of the Poet to Day-Dreaming," *Papers on Metapsychology; Papers on Applied Psycho-Analysis,* trans. Joan Riviere. Vol. 4 of *Collected Papers,* ed. Ernest Jones. The International Psycho-Analytical Library, ed. Ernest Jones, no. 10. London: The Hogarth Press and the Institute of Psycho-Analysis, 1949. Pp. 173–83.

Grant, Douglas. *Walt Whitman and His English Admirers.* Lecture Delivered in the University of Leeds, November 6, 1961. Leeds: Leeds University Press, 1962.

Griffin, William J. "The Use and Abuse of Literature," *Literature and Psychology* 1 (September 1951): 3–20.

Hall, Vernon, Jr. *A Short History of Literary Criticism.* New York: New York University Press, 1963.

Hoffman, Frederick J. *Conrad Aiken.* New York: Twayne Publishers, Inc., 1962.

————. *Freudianism and the Literary Mind.* 1st ed. Baton Rouge: Louisiana State University Press, 1945.

————. *Freudianism and the Literary Mind.* 2d ed. Baton Rouge: Louisiana State University Press, 1957.

————. *Freudianism and the Literary Mind.* First Evergreen Edition. New York: Grove Press, Inc., 1959.

————. "Literary Form and Psychic Tension," in *Hidden Patterns: Studies in Psychoanalytic Literary Criticism,* ed. Leonard and Eleanor Manheim. New York: The Macmillan Company, 1966. Pp. 50–65.

————. "Psychology and Literature," *Literature and Psychology* 6 (1956) : 114–15.

————. "Psychology and Literature," *The Kenyon Review* 19 (Autumn 1957) : 605–19.

————. *The 20's: American Writing in the Postwar Decade.* 2d ed. New York: The Free Press, 1962.

Holloway, Emory. *Whitman, An Interpretation in Narrative.* New York: Alfred A. Knopf, Inc., 1926.

Hubbell, Jay B. "Poe," *Eight American Authors: A Review of Research and Criticism,* ed. Floyd Stovall. New York: W. W. Norton & Company, Inc., 1963. Pp. 1–46.

Hutchens, John K. "One Thing and Another," *Saturday Review* (December 20, 1969) , pp. 24–25.

Hyslop, Lois and Francis E., Jr., trans. and eds. *Baudelaire on Poe*. State College, Pa.: Bald Eagle Press, 1952.

Isaacs, Neil D. "The Autoerotic Metaphor in Joyce, Sterne, Lawrence, Stevens and Whitman," *Literature and Psychology* 15 (Spring 1965) : 92–106.

James, William. *Talks to Teachers on Psychology: and to Students on Some of Life's Ideals*. New York: W. W. Norton & Company, Inc., 1958.

Jones, Ernest. "The Death of Hamlet's Father," *The International Journal of Psycho-Analysis* 29 (1948) : 174–76.

———. *Hamlet and Oedipus*. New York: W. W. Norton and Company, 1949.

———. *The Life and Work of Sigmund Freud*. New York: Basic Books, Inc., 1955. Vol. 2.

Jung, C. G. *The Archetypes and the Collective Unconscious*, trans. R. F. C. Hull. Vol. 9, part 1 of *The Collected Works of C. G. Jung*, Bollingen Series 20, ed. Herbert Read, Michael Fordham, and Gerhard Adler. New York: Pantheon Books Inc., 1959.

———. "The Association Method," trans. A. A. Brill. *American Journal of Psychology* 21 (April 1910) : 219–69.

———. *The Development of Personality*, trans. R. F. C. Hull. Vol. 17 of *Collected Works*. New York: Pantheon Books Inc., 1954.

———. *Modern Man in Search of a Soul*, trans. W. S. Dell and Cary F. Baynes. New York: Harcourt, Brace & World, Inc., 1933.

———. *The Psychogenesis of Mental Disease*, trans. R. F. C. Hull. Vol. 3 of *Collected Works*. New York: Pantheon Books Inc., 1960.

———. *Psychological Types*, trans. H. Godwin Baynes. London: Routledge & Kegan Paul Ltd., 1953.

———. *Symbols of Transformation*, trans. R. F. C. Hull. Vol. 5 of *Collected Works*. New York: Pantheon Books Inc., 1956.

Kanzer, Mark. Review of "Louis Fraiberg—*Psychoanalysis & American Literary Criticism*," *Literature and Psychology* 10 (Spring 1960) : 56–58.

Kazin, Alfred. "Psychoanalysis and Literary Culture Today," *Partisan Review* 16 (Winter 1959): 45–55.

———. "Psychoanalysis and Literary Culture Today," *Psycho-*

analysis and Literature, ed. Hendrik M. Ruitenbeek. New York: E. P. Dutton & Co., Inc., 1964. Pp. 3–13.

Kiell, Norman, comp. and ed. *Psychoanalysis, Psychology and Literature: A Bibliography.* Madison: The University of Wisconsin Press, 1963.

Kris, Ernst, ed. *Psychoanalytic Explorations in Art.* New York: International Universities Press, 1952.

Krutch, Joseph Wood. *Edgar Allan Poe: A Study in Genius.* New York: Alfred A. Knopf, Inc., 1926.

———. *Edgar Allan Poe: A Study in Genius.* New York: Russell & Russell, Inc., 1965.

———. "Genius and Neuroticism," *And Even If You Do.* New York: William Morrow & Company, Inc., 1967. Pp. 145–52.

———. "The Strange Case of Poe," *The American Mercury* 6 (November 1925) : 349–56.

Lauter, Paul. "Walt Whitman: Lover and Comrade," *American Imago* 16 (Winter 1959) : 428–29.

Lawrence, D. H. *Studies in Classic American Literature.* New York: Thomas Seltzer Inc., 1923.

Lemon, Lee T. *The Partial Critics.* New York: Oxford University Press, Inc., 1965.

Levin, Harry. *The Power of Blackness.* New York: Alfred A. Knopf, Inc., 1958.

Lewisohn, Ludwig. *Expression in America.* New York: Harper & Brothers, 1932.

———. *The Story of American Literature.* New York: Modern Library, 1939.

Lindsay, Philip. *The Haunted Man: A Portrait of Edgar Allan Poe.* London: Hutchinson & Co. Ltd., 1953.

Manheim, Leonard and Eleanor, eds. *Hidden Patterns: Studies in Psychoanalytic Literary Criticism.* New York: The Macmillan Company, 1966.

Martin, Jay. *Conrad Aiken: A Life of His Art.* Princeton: Princeton University Press, 1962.

Matthiessen, F. O. *American Renaissance.* New York: Oxford University Press, Inc., 1941.

Miller, Edwin Haviland. *Walt Whitman's Poetry: A Psychological Journey.* Boston: Houghton Mifflin Company, 1968.

Miller, James E., Jr. *A Critical Guide to Leaves of Grass.* Chicago: University of Chicago Press, 1957.

————. *Walt Whitman.* New York: Twayne Publishers, Inc., 1962.

Moore, Marianne. "If A Man Die," *Hound & Horn* 5 (January–March 1932) : 313–20. Reprinted with slight changes in *Wake* 11 (1952) : 50–56.

Murray, Henry A. "Poet of Creative Dissolution," *Wake* 11 (1952) : 95–106.

Pearce, Roy Harvey. *The Continuity of American Poetry.* Princeton: Princeton University Press, 1961.

Peterson, Houston. *The Melody of Chaos.* New York: Longmans, Green and Co., 1931.

Poe, Edgar Allan. "Letter to B—." *Selected Writings of Edgar Allan Poe,* ed. Edward H. Davidson. Boston: Houghton Mifflin Company, 1956. Pp. 409–15.

————. "The Philosophy of Composition," in *The Complete Poems and Stories of Edgar Allan Poe, With Selections from His Critical Writings,* ed. Arthur Hobson Quinn and Edward H. O'Neill. New York: Alfred A. Knopf, Inc., 1951. Vol. 2, pp. 978–87.

————. *The Poems of Edgar Allan Poe,* ed. Floyd Stovall. Charlottesville: The University Press of Virginia, 1965.

Preminger, Alex, ed. *Encyclopedia of Poetry and Poetics.* Princeton: Princeton University Press, 1965. Pp. 158–74.

Prescott, Frederick C. *The Poetic Mind.* Ithaca: Cornell University Press, 1959. (1st ed.: New York: The Macmillan Company, 1922.)

————. "Poetry and Dreams," *Journal of Abnormal Psychology* 7 (April 1912): 17–46, 104–43.

————. *Poetry and Myth.* New York: The Macmillan Company, 1927.

Pruette, Lorine. "A Psycho-Analytical Study of Edgar Allan Poe," *The American Journal of Psychology* 31 (October 1920) : 370–402.

Quinn, Arthur Hobson. *Edgar Allan Poe: A Critical Biography.* New York: D. Appleton-Century Company, Inc., 1941.

Rein, David M. "Conrad Aiken and Psychoanalysis," *The Psychoanalytic Review,* 42, no. 4 (1955) : 402–11.

Robertson, John W. *Edgar A. Poe.* San Francisco: B. Brough, 1921.

Schyberg, Frederik. *Walt Whitman,* trans. Evie Allison Allen. New York: Columbia University Press, 1951.

Sutton, Walter. *Modern American Criticism.* Englewood Cliffs, N.J.: Prentice-Hall, Inc., 1963.

Tate, Allen. "The Author of 'John Deth,' " *The New Republic* 67 (July 22, 1931) : 265–66.

Thorp, Willard. "Walt Whitman," in *Eight American Authors: A Review of Research and Criticism,* ed. Floyd Stovall. New York: W. W. Norton & Company, Inc., 1963. Pp. 271–318.

Untermeyer, Louis. "Conrad Aiken: Our Best Known Unread Poet," *Saturday Review* (November 25, 1967) , pp. 28–29, 76–77.

Van Teslaar, J. S., ed. *An Outline of Psychoanalysis.* New York: The Modern Library, Inc., 1925.

Wells, Henry W. *New Poets from Old: A Study in Literary Genetics.* New York: Columbia University Press, 1940.

Whicher, George F. "The Twentieth Century," in Arthur Hobson Quinn, ed., *The Literature of the American People: An Historical and Critical Survey.* New York: Appleton-Century-Crofts, Inc., 1951. Pp. 813–984.

Whitman, Walt. *Leaves of Grass,* ed. Emory Holloway. Garden City, N.Y.: Doubleday & Company, Inc., 1926.

————. *The Uncollected Poetry and Prose of Walt Whitman,* ed. Emory Holloway. Garden City, N.Y.: Doubleday, Page & Company, 1921.

Wilbur, Robert Hunter. "The Art of Poetry IX: Conrad Aiken —An Interview," Paris Review 11, no. 42 (Winter–Spring 1968) : 97–124.

Winters, Yvor. "Edgar Allan Poe: A Crisis in the History of American Obscurantism," *Maule's Curse: Seven Studies in the History of American Obscurantism.* Norfolk, Conn.: New Directions, 1938. Pp. 93–122.

Winwar, Frances. *American Giant: Walt Whitman and His Times.* New York: Harper & Brothers, 1941.

Young, Philip. "The Earlier Psychologists and Poe," *American Literature* 22 (January 1951) : 442–54.

Index

Adler, Alfred: compensation, 45; "individual psychology," 45; inferiority and superiority complexes, 108n; neurotic constitution, 46n; organic inferiority, 45; *The Practice and Theory of Individual Psychology*, 45n, 49n; *What Life Should Mean to You*, 45n, 49n

Adler, Kurt A., 46n

Aiken, Anna, 85

Aiken, Conrad, 25, 28, 42, 109, 110, 111; concept of beauty and awareness, 94–107; death of parents and influence upon him, 86–87; debt to Freud, 107; psychoanalytic insights into selected poetry, 94–107; quest for identity, 87–89; relationship to depth psychology, 84–94

Aiken, Conrad (Hoffman), 98n, 99

Aiken, Conrad (works): "A Basis for Criticism," 94n, 95; *Blue Voyage*, 86n, 97n; "Changing Mind," 98, 100; "The Charnel Rose," 98, 100; *Collected Poems*, 92n, 98, 101n, 102n, 104n, 106n; *The Coming Forth by Day of Osiris Jones*, 103, 104, 105; *The Divine Pilgrim*, 91, 98, 100; *Earth Triumphant*, 90, 98; "Electra," 101, 102; *Great Circle*, 96, 97n; "The House of Dust," 90, 100; "The Jig of Forslin," 100, 101, 101n; *The Kid*, 88; *King Coffin*, 96, 97n; "The Pilgrimage of Festus,"
91, 92, 100; *Preludes for Memnon*, 89, 103, 104, 105; *Punch: The Immortal Liar*, 90; *Scepticisms*, 90, 100n; *Selected Poems* (1929), 90, 98, 101; *Selected Poems* (1961), 98; "Senlin: A Biography," 100; *Sheepfold Hill: Fifteen Poems*, 100n; "Time in the Rock or Preludes to Definition," 106; *Ushant: An Essay*, 86, 86n, 99, 105

Aiken, William, 85

"Al Aaraaf" (Poe), 56

Allen, Evie Allison, 63n; "A Check List of Whitman Publications 1945–1960," 63n, 72n

Allen, Gay Wilson, 66, 68; *Walt Whitman as Man, Poet, and Legend*, 63n, 65n; *Walt Whitman Handbook*, 67n, 68, 68n

Allen, Hervey, 43n

"Annabel Lee" (Poe), 61

Ansbacher, Heinz L. and Rowena R., eds., *The Individual Psychology of Alfred Adler*, 46n, 49n

Archetypes and the Collective Unconscious, The (Jung), 49n

Aristotle, 95

Art and Psychoanalysis (W. Phillips), 32, 59n

Basic Writings of Sigmund Freud, The (A. A. Brill), 29n, 49n, 55n, 68n, 76n

"Basis for Criticism, A" (Aiken), 94n, 95

Baudelaire, Charles, 59n
Beach, Joseph Warren, 85, 89, 101n
Benchley, Robert, 86n
Bergler, Edmund, 32n
Bergson, Henri, 87
Beyond the Pleasure Principle, Group Psychology, and Other Works (Freud), 26n
Blackmur, R. P., 85, 101, 103
Blanshard, Rufus A., 85, 105
Blue Voyage (Aiken), 86n, 97n
Bonaparte, Marie, 46, 46n, 49n, 53, 56, 57, 59, 62n; *The Life and Works of Edgar Allan Poe: A Psycho-Analytic Interpretation,* 46n, 50n, 53, 59n
Briggs, Arthur E., 66n, 72n
Brill, A. A., 40n, 42n, 57n, 78; *The Basic Writings of Sigmund Freud,* 29n, 49n, 55n, 68n, 76n; "The Introduction of Freud's Work in the United States," 29n
Brooks, Van Wyck, 32
Buranelli, Vincent, 43, 44, 58n; *Edgar Allan Poe,* 44n
Burke, Kenneth, 31, 32, 33, 41, 42
Burnshaw, Stanley, 36, 37, 38, 39
Bychowski, Gustav, 68, 68n, 69, 70, 74, 75, 76, 77, 79, 80, 82; "Walt Whitman: A Study in Sublimation," 71, 74, 75, 77, 80, 81, 82, 83
Byron, Lord George Gordon, 109

Calamus (Whitman), 72, 78
Campbell, Killis, 44n
Canby, Henry Seidel, 63, 64, 66; *Walt Whitman an American,* 64n
Catel, Jean, 66; *Walt Whitman: La Naissance du Poète,* 67
"Changing Mind" (Aiken), 98, 100
"Charnel Rose, The" (Aiken), 98, 100
Chase, Harry W., 29n
Chase, Richard, 64, 79
"Check List of Whitman Publications 1945–1960, A" (E. A. Allen), 63n, 72n

"City in the Sea, The" (Poe), 59, 60
Civilization and Its Discontents (Freud), 48n, 104n
Coleridge, Samuel Taylor, 50
Collected Poems (Aiken), 92n, 98, 101n, 102n, 104n, 106n
Coming Forth by Day of Osiris Jones, The (Aiken), 103, 104, 105
Cooper, James Fenimore, 43
Cowley, Malcolm, 66
Crane, Stephen, 40n
"Creative Writers and Day-Dreaming" (Freud), 34n
Critics and criticism. *See* author and work: *see also* Psychoanalysis and literature, Psychoanalytically oriented literary criticism
Cummings, E. E., 41, 86n

Darwin, Charles Robert, 87, 96
Davidson, Edward H., 47n
da Vinci, Leonardo, 34
Day-dreams/or dreams. *See* Psychoanalytic terms and concepts
Denney, Reuel, 85n
Depth psychology, 46n, 56, 79, 84, 85, 89, 96, 106, 108
de Selincourt, Ernest, 71n
Deutsch, Danica, 46n
Development of Personality, The (Jung), 49n
Dickinson, Emily, 90
Dillon, George, 85, 90, 91, 92, 93; "Mr. Aiken's Poetry," 91n, 93
Divine Pilgrim, The (Aiken), 91, 98, 100
"Dream, A" (Poe), 50, 51, 52
"Dreams" (Poe), 49, 49n, 50n
Dreams. *See* Day-dreams/or dreams
"Dream Within a Dream, A" (Poe), 54, 55
Dreiser, Theodore, 40n
Dynamic psychology, 24, 38, 89

Earth Triumphant (Aiken), 90, 98
Edel, Leon, 24n
Edwards, Jonathan, 43

Ego psychology, 32, 110
"Electra" (Aiken), 101, 102
Eliot, T. S., 41, 86n, 91; "The Wasteland," 101n
Encyclopedia of Poetry and Poetics (Preminger), 40n
Existentialism, 89
Expression in America (Lewisohn), 40, 41

"Fall of the House of Usher, The" (Poe), 58n
Faulkner, William, 43
Ferenczi, S., 69n
Fodor, Nandor, 68n, 69n
Foerster, Norman, 48, 48n
Fraiberg, Louis, 32, 33, 33n; *Psychoanalysis and American Literary Criticism*, 26n, 32, 33n
Freudianism and the Literary Mind (Hoffman), 30, 31, 40n, 97n
Freud, Sigmund, 23, 26–27, 29–42, 42n, 46, 46n, 47n, 51n, 53, 53n, 60n, 64n, 65, 68n, 69n, 84, 85, 87, 95, 96, 97n, 99, 103, 106n, 107, 108, 108n; influences upon development of his theories, 23; lectures at Clark University, 29–30
Freud, Sigmund (works): *Beyond the Pleasure Principle, Group Psychology, and Other Works*, 26n; *Civilization and Its Discontents*, 48n, 104n; "Creative Writers and Day-Dreaming," 34n; *A General Introduction to Psycho-Analysis*, 53n, 57n, 78n; *Group Psychology and the Analysis of the Ego*, 69n; "History of the Psychoanalytic Movement," 29n; "The Interpretation of Dreams," 48n, 49n, 55n, 60n, 76n; *The Interpretation of Dreams (I)*, 49n; *The Interpretation of Dreams (II) and On Dreams*, 49n; *Leonardo da Vinci*, 57n; *Moses and Monotheism*, 57n; *New Introductory Lectures on Psycho-Analysis*, 52n, 70n; "On the History of the Psycho-Analytic Movement," 30n; "Psycho-Analysis," 26n; "The Relation of the Poet to Day-Dreaming," 34, 34n, 50n, 64n

Gaynor, Frank, 68n, 69n
General Introduction to Psycho-Analysis, A (Freud), 53n, 57n, 78n
Goethe, Johann Wolfgang von, 34
Grant, Douglas, 80
Great Circle (Aiken), 96, 97n
Griffin, William J., 24n
Group Psychology and the Analysis of the Ego (Freud), 69n

Hall, G. Stanley, 29
Hall, Vernon, Jr., 108n
Hamlet (Shakespeare), 31, 34
Hamlet and Oedipus (E. Jones), 31
Hawthorne, Nathaniel, 40n, 43
Heine, Heinrich, 109
Hemingway, Ernest, 44
Hidden Patterns: Studies in Psychoanalytic Literary Criticism (L. and E. Manheim), 31n, 33
"History of the Psychoanalytic Movement" (Freud), 29n
Hoffman, Frederick J., 31, 85, 97, 98, 106; *Conrad Aiken*, 98n, 99; *Freudianism and the Literary Mind*, 30, 31, 40n, 97n; "Peripheries of Literature," 31; *Psychology and Literature*, 31, 31n; *The 20's: American Writing in the Postwar Decade*, 97n
Holloway, Emory, 66n, 67; *Uncollected Poetry and Prose of Walt Whitman*, 67; *Whitman, An Interpretation in Narrative*, 67
"House of Dust, The" (Aiken), 90, 100
Hubbell, Jay B., 43n
Hugo, Victor, 109
Hutchens, John K., 106n

Hyslop, Francis E., Jr., and Lois, 59n

Individual Psychology of Alfred Adler, The (H. and R. Ansbacher), 46n, 49n
"Interpretation of Dreams, The" (Freud), 48n, 49n, 55n, 60n, 76n
Interpretation of Dreams, The (I) (Freud), 49n
Interpretation of Dreams, The (II) and On Dreams (Freud), 49n
"Introduction of Freud's Work in the United States, The" (A. A. Brill), 29n
Isaacs, Neil D., 74, 75
"I Sing the Body Electric" (Whitman), 80
"Israfel" (Poe), 57, 58n

James, Henry, 40n
James, William, 30n, 71n
"Jig of Forslin, The" (Aiken), 100, 101, 101n
Jones, Ernest, 26n, 30n, 32, 34n, 50n, 64n, 69n; Hamlet and Oedipus, 31; The Life and Work of Sigmund Freud, 29n
Joyce, James, 97n
Jung, Carl Gustav, 29, 29n, 36, 38, 39, 40, 108, 108n; lectures at Clark University, 29
Jung, Carl Gustav (works): The Archetypes and the Collective Unconscious, 49n; The Development of Personality, 49n; Modern Man in Search of a Soul, 36n; The Psychogenesis of Mental Disease, 49n; Psychological Types, 38n; Symbols of Transformation, 49n

Kanzer, Mark, 33n
Kazin, Alfred, 85, 96, 106
Keats, John, 50, 109
Keble, Reverend John, 39
Kid, The (Aiken), 88
Kiell, Norman, ed., Psychoanalysis,

Psychology and Literature: A Bibliography, 30n
King Coffin (Aiken), 96, 97n
Kris, Ernst, ed., Psychoanalytic Explorations in Art, 31, 32
Krutch, Joseph Wood, 32, 47n, 50, 50n, 59n, 62n

Lauter, Paul, 72, 79: "Walt Whitman: Lover and Comrade," 78
Lawrence, D. H., 40n, 75, 81n; Studies in Classic American Literature, 58n, 75n, 81
Leaves of Grass (Whitman), 63, 66, 68, 69, 70, 71, 72, 74, 76, 77, 81–82
Lemon, Lee T., 26; The Partial Critics, 26n
Leonard, William Ellery, 41
Leonardo da Vinci (Freud), 57n
"Leonore" (Poe), 61
Leopardi, Giacomo, 109
Lermontov, Mikhail Yurevich, 109
"Letter to B —" (Poe), 47n
Levin, Harry, 53n, 58n
Lewisohn, Ludwig, 32, 40n, 41; Expression in America, 40, 41; The Story of American Literature, 40
Life and Works of Edgar Allan Poe: A Psycho-Analytic Interpretation, The (Bonaparte), 46n, 50n, 53, 59n
Life and Work of Sigmund Freud, The (E. Jones), 29n
Lindsay, Philip, 44
Lindsay, Vachel, 41
Lippmann, Walter, 86n
Literary criticism. See Psychoanalytically oriented literary criticism
Literature and psychoanalysis. See Psychoanalysis and literature

Manheim, Leonard and Eleanor, eds., Hidden Patterns: Studies in Psychoanalytic Literary Criticism, 31n, 33
Martin, Jay, 86n

Marx, Karl, 96
Maslow, Abraham, 83
Matthiessen, F. O., 50n, 80n
McCouch, Dr. G. P., 97n
Melody of Chaos, The (Peterson), 86n, 87, 89, 101n
Melville, Herman, 40n, 43, 93
Michelangelo, 34
Miller, Edwin Haviland, 64n
Miller, James, Jr., 72, 81n
Modern American Criticism (Sutton), 33n, 41
Modern Man in Search of a Soul (Jung), 36n
Moore, Marianne, 85, 104
Moses, 34
Moses and Monotheism (Freud), 57n
"Mr. Aiken's Poetry" (Dillon), 91n, 93
Muller, Herbert J., 37, 38
Murray, Henry A., 85, 92, 93, 94, 106; "Poet of Creative Dissolution," 93n, 96

National Medal for Literature (Aiken), 106n
New Introductory Lectures on Psycho-Analysis (Freud), 52n, 70n
Nietzsche, Friedrich Wilhelm, 87
Norris, Frank, 40n

Oedipus Rex (Sophocles), 31
"Of the Terrible Doubt of Appearances" (Whitman), 71, 72, 75
Old Testament, 109
O'Neill, Edward H., 54n, 62n
"On the History of the Psycho-Analytic Movement" (Freud), 30n
"Out of the Cradle Endlessly Rocking" (Whitman), 73, 74, 75
Oxford movement, 39

Partial Critics, The (Lemon), 26n
Pearce, Roy Harvey, 60, 85, 88
"Peripheries of Literature" (Hoffman), 31

Peterson, Houston, 85; *The Melody of Chaos*, 86n, 87, 89, 101n
Phillips, William, ed., *Art and Psychoanalysis*, 32, 59n
"Philosophy of Composition, The" (Poe), 54n
"Pilgrimage of Festus, The" (Aiken), 91, 92, 100
Poe, Edgar Allan, 25, 27, 28, 40n, 42, 43–62, 84, 85, 109, 110, 111; psychoanalytic attempts to study his personality, 43–46; psychoanalytically oriented criticism of selected poetry, 47–62; rationale of poetry, 47
Poe, Edgar Allan (Buranelli), 44n
Poe, Edgar Allan (works): "Al Aaraaf," 56; "Annabel Lee," 61; "The City in the Sea," 59, 60; "A Dream," 50, 51, 52; "A Dream Within a Dream," 54, 55; "Dreams," 49, 49n, 50n; "The Fall of the House of Usher," 58n; "Israfel," 57, 58n; "Leonore," 61; "Letter to B —," 47n; "The Philosophy of Composition," 54n; "The Raven," 53, 61; "The Sleeper," 60, 61; "Sonnet—To Science," 52; "Sonnet to Zante," 61; *Tamerlane and Other Poems*, 49n; "To One in Paradise," 61; "Ulalume," 61; *William Wilson*, 45
Poe, Virginia, 62
Poems of Edgar Allan Poe, The (Stovall), 49n
"Poet of Creative Dissolution" (Murray), 93n, 96
Poetic Mind, The (Prescott), 37, 37n, 38, 39
"Poetry and Dreams" (Prescott), 36n, 37
Poets and poetry. See individual poet and work
Porter, Alan, 45n, 49n
Pound, Ezra, 41
Practice and Theory of Individual Psychology, The (Adler), 45n, 49n

Prelude, The (Wordsworth) , 91
Preludes for Memnon (Aiken) , 89,
    103, 104, 105
Preminger, Alex, *Encyclopedia of
    Poetry and Poetics*, 40n
Prescott, Frederick C., 37, 38n, 39,
    39n, 40n; *The Poetic Mind*, 37,
    37n, 38, 39; "Poetry and Dreams,"
    36n, 37
Proust, Marcel, 93
Pruette, Lorine, 45, 46, 46n, 51,
    57, 61, 62; "A Psycho-Analytical
    Study of Edgar Allan Poe," 48,
    55, 60
"Psycho-Analysis" (Freud) , 26n
*Psychoanalysis and American Lit-
    erary Criticism* (Fraiberg) , 26n,
    32, 33n
Psychoanalysis and literature: and
    critical judgment, 31; and poetry,
    34–42; approaches to poetry
    (Freud and Jung) , 36; influence
    of classical Freudian psycho-
    analysis, 32; rationale and sub-
    ject matter, 24; relationship, 24
*Psychoanalysis, Psychology and Lit-
    erature: A Bibliography* (Kiell) ,
    30n
Psychoanalytic Explorations in Art
    (Kris) , 31, 32
Psychoanalytic terms and concepts:
    beauty, 47n, 48, 48n, 61, 94, 95;
    catharsis, 39; collective uncon-
    scious, 38n, 108n; compensation,
    45; conscious, 32, 38n, 59, 68,
    100, 109; consciousness, 72, 91,
    94, 103, 104; day-dreams/or
    dreams, 34, 35, 36, 39, 40, 48,
    48n, 49, 49n, 50, 50n, 51, 53, 55,
    55n, 58, 59, 60, 64n, 85, 95, 100,
    110; death-wishes, 60; defense
    mechanisms, 110; displacement,
    59, 110; dream interpretation, 39;
    ego, 47n, 69, 69n, 70n, 71, 74,
    77, 79, 82, 83; "Electra," 34;
    guilt feelings, 79; identification,
    69, 69n, 70, 70n, 78n, 83, 110;
    infantile experiences, 46; infan-
    tile repressions, 79; inferiority

and superiority complexes, 108n;
    introjection, 69, 69n, 110; narcis-
    sism, 77, 78, 78n, 83; newer
    concepts, 106n; Oedipal theme,
    99, 110; "Oedipus," 34; Oedipus
    complex, 26; omnipotence, 50n,
    95, 110; "phantasy," 34, 35, 38n,
    64n; pleasure, 47n, 48, 48n;
    pleasure-principle, 53n, 58, 110;
    pleasure and unpleasure, 47n;
    psychoanalytic theory, 23, 26, 33,
    102, 103, 110; "racial memories,"
    39; reality principle, 53n, 110;
    repression, 26, 35, 80, 89, 94, 110;
    resistance, 26, 110; sexual in-
    stinct, 69n; sexuality, 26, 110;
    subconscious, 100; sublimation,
    68, 68n, 69, 79, 80, 110; uncon-
    scious, 26, 35, 38, 38n, 39, 40, 53,
    59, 68, 74, 75, 100, 103, 108n,
    109, 110; wish-fulfillment, 34, 35,
    39, 41, 50, 50n, 53, 55n, 58, 95,
    100
Psychoanalytically oriented criti-
    cism. *See* Psychoanalysis and
    literature. *See also* Psychoana-
    lytically oriented literary criti-
    cism
Psychoanalytically oriented literary
    criticism: basic tools, 40; dangers
    of, 44; definition and elaboration,
    26; function of good criticism,
    33; in United States, 31–34;
    limitations, 27; use of term, 25
"Psycho-Analytical Study of Edgar
    Allan Poe, A" (Pruette) , 48, 55,
    60
*Psychogenesis of Mental Disease,
    The* (Jung) , 49n
Psychological Types (Jung) , 38n
Psychology and Literature (Hoff-
    man) , 31, 31n
Pulitzer Prize (Aiken) , 90, 98
Punch: The Immortal Liar
    (Aiken) , 90

Quinn, Arthur Hobson, 43n, 54n,
    62n, 90n

"Raven, The" (Poe), 53, 61

Reed, John, 86n

Rein, David M., 85, 99, 99n, 100, 101, 106

"Relation of the Poet to Day-Dreaming, The" (Freud), 34, 34n, 50n, 64n

Robertson, Dr. John W., 46n, 47n, 62n

Robinson, E. A., 41

Róheim, Géza, 68n

Ruitenbeek, Hendrik M., 41n, 97n

Sachs, Hanns, 32

Santayana, George, 87

Scepticisms (Aiken), 90, 100n

Schyberg, Frederik, 66, 72

Selected Poems (Aiken): (1929), 90, 98, 101; (1961), 98

"Senlin: A Biography" (Aiken), 100

Shakespeare, William, *Hamlet*, 31, 34

Sheepfold Hill: Fifteen Poems (Aiken), 100n

Shelley, Percy Bysshe, 50, 109

"Sleeper, The" (Poe), 60, 61

"So Long" (Whitman), 65, 66

"Song of Myself" (Whitman), 66, 77, 78, 79, 80

"Song of the Open Road" (Whitman), 81n

"Sonnet—To Science" (Poe), 52

"Sonnet to Zante" (Poe), 61

Sophocles, *Oedipus Rex*, 31

Stanard, Mrs. Helen, 62

"Starting from Paumanok" (Whitman), 81, 82

Stekel, W., 55n

Sterba, Dr. Richard, 100n

St. Mary's sermon, 39

Story of American Literature, The (Lewisohn), 40

Stovall, Floyd, 43n, 51, 52, 55, 56, 57n, 58, 60, 61, 63n; *The Poems of Edgar Allan Poe*, 49n

Strachey, James, 26n, 30n, 34n, 48n, 49n, 69n, 104n

Studies in Classic American Literature (Lawrence), 58n, 75n, 81

Sutton, Walter, *Modern American Criticism*, 33n, 41

Symbols of Transformation (Jung), 49n

Tamerlane and Other Poems (Poe), 49n

Tate, Allan, 101n

The 20's: American Writing in the Postwar Decade (Hoffman), 97n

"There Was a Child Went Forth" (Whitman), 69, 70

Thorp, Willard, 63n

"Time in the Rock or Preludes to Definition" (Aiken), 106

"To One in Paradise" (Poe), 61

"To Think of Time" (Whitman), 76

Trilling, Lionel, 32, 33

"Ulalume" (Poe), 61

Uncollected Poetry and Prose of Walt Whitman (Holloway), 67

University of Georgia Press, 98

Untermeyer, Louis, 84, 85n

Ushant: An Essay (Aiken), 86, 86n, 99, 105

Van O'Connor, William, 37, 38, 89n

Van Teslaar, J. S., 69n

"Walt Whitman: A Study in Sublimation" (Bychowski), 71, 74, 75, 77, 80, 81, 82, 83

Walt Whitman an American (Canby), 64n

Walt Whitman as Man, Poet, and Legend (G. W. Allen), 63n, 65n

Walt Whitman Handbook (G. W. Allen), 67n, 68, 68n

Walt Whitman: La Naissance du Poète (Catel), 67

"Walt Whitman: Lover and Comrade" (Lauter), 78

"Wasteland, The" (Eliot), 101n

Wells, Henry W., 85, 87, 88

What Life Should Mean to You (Adler), 45n, 49n

Whicher, George F., 85, 90

Whitman, An Interpretation in Narrative (Holloway), 67

Whitman, Walt, 25, 28, 40n, 42, 50n, 63–83, 84, 109, 110, 111; psychoanalytically oriented criticism of selected poetry, 68–83; psychodynamic considerations, 63–68

Whitman, Walt (works) : *Calamus*, 72, 78; "I Sing the Body Electric," 80; *Leaves of Grass*, 63, 66, 68, 69, 70, 71, 72, 74, 76, 77, 81, 82; "Of the Terrible Doubt of Appearances," 71, 72, 75; "Out of the Cradle Endlessly Rocking," 73, 74, 75; "So Long,"

65, 66; "Song of Myself," 66, 77, 78, 79, 80; "Song of the Open Road," 81n; "Starting from Paumanok," 81, 82; "There Was a Child Went Forth," 69, 70; "To Think of Time," 76

Wilbur, Robert Hunter, 106n

William Wilson (Poe), 45

Williams, William Carlos, 41

Wilson, Edmund, 31, 32, 33

Winters, Yvor, 48n

Winwar, Frances, 81n, 82

Wordsworth, William, *The Prelude*, 91

Young, Philip, 47n

This exploratory study of selected criticism of selected poems by Poe, Whitman, and Aiken will help point up for the whole genre of poetry the value and the limitation of literary criticism that has a psychoanalytical orientation. These poets have been chosen as typical, for, like poets of all time, they treat the familiar themes of birth, life, death, love, beauty, faith, hope, fear, anxiety, and many another human emotion and experience. Furthermore, each of the three poets has worked within a particular tradition.

Edgar Allan Poe writes within the romantic tradition made familiar by Byron, Keats, Shelley, Hugo, Heine, Leopardi, and Lermontov, to name a few. He may be said to have dived into the tidal wave of the romantic movement after it had established itself in Europe and was beginning to make itself felt in American literature.

Walt Whitman vaunts the rising exuberance of a growing America as he sings of himself with utter abandon and sweeping freedom. There is a deep biblical strain in his poems, reminiscent of Hebrew poetry in the Old Testament.

Conrad Aiken's poetry seems constantly to strive toward perfect symphonic arrangement; he aims to reevoke the closer relationship between poetry and music, very much in the tradition of the Greek tragic chorus. In concerning him-